Strength-Based Empowerment Theory™

A Model for Lifting the Spirit,
Reprogramming the Mind,
Instilling Self-Love, and
Developing Self-Reliance in
African American Male Offenders

Jerry E. Smith, Jr., MA
Kimm C. Hurley-Smith, MSW, LCSW

Published by KHU Consulting Services

For further information:
KHU Consulting Services
7426 Cherry Avenue,
Suite 210-412
Fontana, CA (92336)
909-331-0697
www.linkstoempowerment.com

ISBN: 1-4392-0077-7
ISBN-13: 9781439200773

Visit www.booksurge.com to order additional copies.
Babyletstalk.com

DEDICATION

In writing this book, I am reminded of my baby brother, Michael Thomas Smith, whose life was cut short by the hands of other human beings at the age of thirty-two. The authorities of Decatur, Illinois, have not brought the perpetrators to justice. I dedicate this book to his memory and all he could have been. My work with offenders has been a cleansing process for me. My goal is to help offenders discover and commit to a healthier, more productive, crime-free way of life.

I also dedicate this work to our oldest son, Jermaine Jerold Smith (JJ), who passed with cancer on November 22, 2006, at the age of thirty-two. He fought courageously for three plus years as he did in life, overcoming obstacles and rising to a higher level of understanding that cultivated him into becoming a better husband, father, son and citizen. He made us proud. His stay on earth is forever etched in our hearts and memories. He epitomizes the principles of this work.

TABLE OF CONTENTS

PART 1: THE PHILOSOPHY

PART 2: AFRICAN-CENTERED TREATMENT

PART 3: THE LINKS OF EMPOWERMENT

PART 4: THE CIRCLE OF EMPOWERMENT

FOREWORD

Considering what is relevant, appropriate and effective as it relates to behavioral changes with incarcerated men of African ancestry, the pioneering and innovative strength based empowerment theory by Jerry and Kimm Smith provides a valuable template for manhood development for this population. Their model espouses with clarity a step-by-step, user-friendly program model with specific emphasis on identifying, utilizing and capitalizing on accentuating the inherent positive strengths, qualities, attributes, abilities and skill levels that are often dormant or ignored in the lives of black African incarcerated males.

Commissioners, wardens, facility and unit directors, wing supervisors and other practitioners working within the field of adult and juvenile corrections rarely have access to program intervention models that resonate and connect in significantly meaningful ways with inmates/residents of black African ancestry. The search for appropriate tools to address the needs of this population is an ongoing challenge that will be addressed with the model set forth in this book.

Despite arguments and proclamations by individuals such as Martinson (1974) that programs have minimal impact on behavioral changes of incarcerated persons, much empirical data and studies have evolved to the contrary. The studies by Andrews, et. al. (1990) and Lipsey (1992) document a fifteen to thirty percent reduction in recidivism of offenders who receive rehabilitative programming compared to those who do not. Further documentation can be found in the work of Cullen (2002), Gendreau, Goggin, Cullen and Andrews (2000) and Petersillia to support the value of providing rehabilitative programs to combat recidivism.

Jerry and Kimm Smith have developed a model that places major emphasis on the offender becoming knowledgeable about his history and culture in positive ways. The offender is led to take initial steps towards becoming self-empowered by facing who they genuinely are as men of African ancestry within a history and culture that portrays them as a proud people rather than being an object of ridicule. Having an opportunity to appreciate this level of knowledge has the potential to gradually propel offenders to look closely at themselves as they choose to adopt more humanistic mannerisms for living in greater harmony with others. In the process, acquiring this newfound understanding and appreciation of self-empowerment will encourage inmates/residents to gain a fuller appreciation for the principles of self-love, self-control, personal accountability, manhood development, decision making, perseverance, goal setting, collective unity and spirituality (belief in a supreme being). These are the values and principles that place a high premium on living a life that is based on an African-centered value system.

The authors' conceptual and evidence-based African-centered paradigm skillfully incorporates the research, scholarship and practice of some of the preeminent African-centered historians, psychologists, educators, theologians/spiritual leaders, and criminal justice practitioners.

The strength based empowerment model is steeped in the African-centered values system of both Kemetic (Ancient Egyptian) virtues of MAAT: *ORDER, BALANCE, HARMONY, TRUTH, JUSTICE, RECIPROCITY* and *PROPRIETY* as well as Dr. Maulana Karenga's Seven Principles of blackness, the NGUZO-SABA: *UNITY, SELF-DETERMINATION, COLLECTIVE WORK AND RESPONSIBILITY, COOPERATIVE ECONOMICS, PURPOSE, CREATIVITY* and *FAITH.*

This strength based empowerment model clearly reflects the astute experiential knowledge that the authors have acquired and have articulated as a result of their work for many years in institutional settings, aftercare probation sites, and with black African American males who exhibited significant aggressive tendencies. It is with these facts in mind that this timely work is regarded as worthy of being instituted in any and all correctional institutions where there are black males of African ancestry. The state of Wisconsin is an ideal starting point for the institutional impetus of utilizing not only the model, but also having its authors as the source for continued study and replication on behalf of a population that is in dire need of a paradigm shift and our society that must address the cause and impact of criminal behavior on our communities.

Strength based empowerment theory promises to enhance programming, assist with inmate/resident/staff safety, and, in the long run, help develop responsible men who can be readmitted to their communities as self-empowered and positively re-socialized with greater self-awareness and skills for integrating back into their families and communities.

As former commissioner of the third largest juvenile justice system in the United States of America, my thoughts of utilizing a model such as this one are twofold: (1) the concept of providing strength-based opportunities considering the racial and ethnic component is not a novel one, but surely having the concept instituted as a collective entity model for the purpose of elevating one's thoughts towards empowerment holds so much logic for success; (2) my belief that all people have the capacity to change is further validated by this model that seeks out positive rather than pathological reasons for making choices and decisions. With this in view as I reflect on my tenure as commissioner of the previously known NYS Division for Youth, I can only regret that I did not have the opportunity to institute this strength-based model as a pivotal program for addressing our goal for deterring recidivism among the inmate/resident population.

> Leonard G. Dunston, MSW
> V.P. Preudhomme, Dunston and
> Associates Consulting and Training Co.

Leonard G. Dunston served as Commissioner, New York State Division for Youth (currently the Office of Children and Family Services) for twelve years. He is highly regarded for having served in this capacity for the longest term in the history of the agency. Mr. Dunston is a past president of the National Association of Black Social Workers, Inc. Currently, Mr. Dunston serves on several boards including; Institute of the Black World, 21st Century, The Harvest Institute, and The National Black Leadership Commission on AIDS. He is semi-retired following twenty-nine years of public service in New York and North Carolina. Mr. Dunston resides in Durham, North Carolina.

ENDNOTES

Martinson, R. (1974). What Works? Questions and answers about prison reform. The Public Interest, pg. 35, 22–54.

Andrews, D., Zinger, Hoge, R., Bonta, J., Gendreau, P., & Cullen, F. (1990 b). Does Correctional Treatment Work? A clinically relevant and psychologically informed meta-analysis. Criminology, pg. 28, 367–404.

Lipsey, M. W. (1992). Juvenile Delinquency Treatment: A meta-analytic inquiry into the variability of effects. In T.D. Cook, H. Cooper, D.S. Corday, H. Hartmann, L.V. Hedges, R.J. Light, et. al. (Eds.), meta-analysis for explanation: a casebook (pg. 83–127) New York: Russell Sage.

Cullen, F. (2002). Rehabilitation and treatment programs. In J. Wilson and J. Petersilia (Eds.) Crime: Public policies for crime control (2nd ed., pg. 253–289). Oakland, CA, ICS: Press.

Gendreau, P., Goggin, C., Cullen, F., and Andrews, D. (2000). The effects of community sanctions and incarceration on recidivism. Forum on Corrections Research, p 12, 10–13.

Petersilia, J. (2003). When prisoners come home: Parole and prisoner reentry. Oxford, U. K.: Oxford University Press.

PREFACE

LIFE'S LESSONS

Repeating, repeating, the lessons of life

Reappearing, reappearing, the lessons of life

Revealing the lessons of life

Piercing the soul, charring the heart, annoying sanity

Life's lessons

Recapitulating, recapitulating, the lessons of life

Reforming, reforming, the lessons of life

Capturing my hopes, strangling my motivation
Resuscitating my pain, my failures, my disappointments
Betraying my trust, discounting my value

Life's lessons

Turning the corner, hoping for the best

Reaching for understanding, meeting success—short lived

Turned back to pain, failure, disappointment,

Starting again, with tattered confidence, fragile hope, frail motivation

Depleted capacity, disconcerted, isolated,

Life's lessons

Sounding the alarm, pronouncing the declaration
of homicidal
Corralling sinister, heinous thoughts, feelings

Amenable to terminating life, searching for removal
Shocked by the internment of victimization

Rebelling against forgiveness, responsibility, accountability
Justifying the retaliation, fueling the desperation
for revenge

Life's lessons

Collapsing the misery

Conquering the lessons in life

Reaffirming, reforming, the lessons of life

Choosing my achievements, my abilities, my happiness

Life's lessons become lessons, not mandates, just
experiences to shape my life

Life's lessons are my gems to discover, to apply effectively
for my success, for my peace of mind

That's life's lessons, seeds for your planting, for your
cultivating, for your harvest

In the key of life—life's lessons!

Jerry E. Smith, Jr. **2002**

I started my career in education as a junior high school counselor and civil rights enforcement, affirmative action, and finally to corrections. In 2004, I retired from the State of Wisconsin after twenty-seven years of service, seventeen in the Department of Corrections as a parole commission member, associate warden, chairperson of the Parole Commission, treatment director, and corrections field supervisor. At the age of fifty-five, I had to complete agent basic training, which included being sprayed with pepper spray—what an experience!

In corrections, I found myself a custodian of human beings, and from that, an advocate for human rights. I was in the position of determining who would be released from prison, which offered me the opportunity to use my training and advocacy skills. However, I continued to feel less than whole and felt disconnected from something greater than myself. I felt detached from my life's commitment of providing a positive bridge for others to cross in order to achieve their positive goals and fulfillment.

The correctional environment began to sap my energy, hope, and excitement for mankind, and dampened my enthusiasm for avenging the blight of hopelessness, fatalism, internalized racism, and self-destruction. I saw on the faces, in the eyes, and heard in the voices of African American men the repressive environment of prison life a tragedy of epic proportions. This book reflects the culmination of my desire to be a vehicle and a voice that lifts men.

As the Chair of the Parole Commission and as a Commissioner, I determined who was paroled from prison. I supervised offenders in the community, served on the school board, spent many years cultivating the group process, spoke to inmate groups on the empowerment model, and oversaw treatment for incarcerated males. My extensive research, experience, and knowledge combined with that of my co-author, Kimm C. Hurley-Smith, created a blueprint for influencing a positive change in the decision-making and behavior of African American male offenders through the strength-based empowerment theory.

Co-author Hurley-Smith has worked with the prison and juvenile populations throughout her career. She has had extensive experience with the California Department of Corrections and the Federal prison system probation and parole. She developed pre-release programs for the department that prepared both men and women for successful reentry into society. These programs covered drug and alcohol addiction, domestic violence, self-esteem, the world of work, and family relationships. Further, as a consultant she developed training programs for correctional officers specifically geared toward those working with African American male inmates.

As a trained licensed mental health practitioner, Hurley-Smith facilitated groups for male offenders who were on state and federal probation. Using a variety of assessment tools, she wrote extensive psychological reports to probation officers regarding the mental health of ex-offenders. These reports included recommendations concerning the offender's probation status.

Our current work together has included designing empowerment groups for offenders. Using history, self knowledge, music and relationships, we worked with many groups in the State of Wisconsin to develop their responsibility to themselves. We discuss emotional pain and perceived failure, from an African-centered perspective, in the context of strength and encouragement. The letters we receive from this work reflect how the inmates internalize the message to redefine themselves, and consequently, make better use of their time during incarceration. Many letters reveal their longing for a stronger family connection. Other letters speak to their lack of opportunity in the prison to be anything other than a barber or janitor; they were disappointed with the programs and training. They felt more than trapped in not being able to be anything other than a caged human being.

In 1991, I began working with the Wisconsin Circle of Recovery in the Wisconsin Prison System. This support group for African American male offenders was comprised of rituals, spirituality, unity, and a specific connection with the history and culture of African Americans. Amos N. Wilson, author of The Falsification of African Consciousness [1] professes that through studying the history of Africans and African Americans, we come to understand ourselves as individuals and as a people. Therefore, our treatment model is "African-centered." However, it is applicable to all offenders in the United States prison system and to other target populations in various social institutions as well. In the Circle of Recovery groups there were men from various ethnic and cultural groups.

Early on in this work, I realized the group structure was needed to maximize the effort and enhance the goal setting and achievement of the group for the individual participants. Group structure would also foster good habits, effectively harness the talents, abilities, develop leadership among the group participants, and provide for orderly and productive meetings. The goal of the groups is to add meaningful introspection, and promote actual healing of the soul. After several years of my earlier work with the group and working with my co-author, the strength-based empowerment theory was born.

Our theoretic model identifies and employs the **strengths** of African American males to develop realistic and practical rehabilitation strategies. The treatment process is culturally specific. Following Na'im Akbar's[2] prescription for diminishing the plague of self-destruction, the strength-based empowerment theory strives to affirm cultural identity, lift up African American values and promote the idea of collective freedom. The strength-based empowerment theory recognizes that the plight, existence, recovery, and survival of African American males are unique from other offenders. Mears and Kahan[3] recognize this unique experience in noting that proactive policing focuses on "the incarceration of geographically concentrated, low-level dealers inevitably lead[ing] to family disruption, unemployment, and low economic status—all of which create social disorganization." The strength-based empowerment theory rests on the premise that the African American male offender's success is linked to his knowledge, understanding, appreciation and commitment to his history, self-acknowledgement, self-love, personal accountability, and unity. It emphasizes strategies and models for living a responsible life from an African perspective that encourages individuals to see themselves as part of something greater.

The strength-based empowerment theory encourages African American male offenders to know who they are and to understand their thinking process by identifying feelings, which can help them to control their actions. Na'im Akbar reminds us, "...your actions follow your mind." (Breaking the Chains of Psychological Slavery, page 58, 1996). The goal is to direct their talents, abilities, and strengths to achieve and maintain positive results whether they are released from prison or not.

The equation for the strength-based empowerment theory is:

Belonging + Outcome + Safety + Spirituality **(BOSS)** = Circle of Empowerment + African American Male Offender + African Centered Treatment + Links of Empowerment **(CALL)** = Crime-Free, African American Offender, Responsible, Empowering, Self-actualized......[member of society] **(CARES)**

BOSS represents the areas in which each offender develops competency through CALL, and they are empowered to achieve the personal development level of CARES. BOSS enables the offender to be the steward of his life in a productive way that generates positive results and habits. Through the mastery of BOSS techniques and strategies, the offender becomes aware of his internal psychological areas of deficiencies that render him ill-equipped to navigate and manage successfully the demands of daily living.

CALL represents the pathways that the offender uses to get to CARES—the pinnacle of achievement that enables the offender to live an empowering life, to employ empowering thinking, to generate empowering thoughts, to use the tools of empowerment, to take empowering action, and to apply empowering reinforcement. The offender becomes the entrepreneur of his life's design. The offender cares about himself, his family, and his community in healthy ways. He removes the shackles of victimization and predator to standing on the solid ground of believing in himself, committing to being a positive contributor, and assuming personal responsibility for himself.

The persuasions of politicians and the unchallenged systemic conditions of society have populated the prisons and jails with African American males. One of the goals for individuals in The Covenant with Black America is to "hold all leaders and elected officials responsible and demand that they change current policy" (page 56).

This proclivity for appearing to get tough on crime has created a financial and human cost of untold proportions. Recidivism and incarceration rates have depleted educational resources, separated families, caused the incarceration of more juveniles as adults, and provided the illusion of safer communities, while releasing offenders with less rehabilitative tools, knowledge, and skills to contribute to safe communities.

On one hand we have public policy purporting progress, while legislation and budget cuts cause adverse effects. Children, the elderly, families, and the poor are in greater peril than ever before. This spiraling conglomeration of meanness has not produced the positive results of less recidivism, less imprisonment, and safer communities. We have more police officers being added to the streets while jobs continue to go oversees and to the suburbs, away from the most challenged families, schools, and communities.

This story describes an actual experience where I observed a meeting in which one of the institutional liaison agents I supervised and an inmate were planning for his release to the community. This particular offender was an African America male who was a high school graduate, had no prior criminal record, he began using drugs he had given up on life. He also indicated that he was sure his long-term relationship with his girlfriend had ended since she did not write or visit him. He did not want to live in a halfway house because he felt the rules were too restrictive. He then asked about getting permission to travel out of state to visit his son in Chicago.

During our interview, I decided to share some insight with him. I asked him what a halfway house had to do with his restrictions when it is the mind that restricts progress, not rules or a building. I suggested that he concentrate on his goal of remaining crime-free and being a contributing member of society and look at the halfway house as the Creator's way of preparing him for those goals. I indicated that if a person concentrates on barriers he fails to see the opportunities. I posed to him that a father is one who is involved intimately and consistently in the life of his child, and that personal sacrifices are normal when it comes to meeting the needs of your child/ren. I suggested that he use whatever means necessary to see his child as an important part of showing the child that he truly has a father who cares.

His comments and mannerisms showed that he was unsure of himself. I reminded him that he is made in the image of the Creator, which makes him as valuable as Michael Jordan or Colin Powell or any other figure that he admires. I suggested that how we see ourselves is going to determine how we see our mind, body and soul. I informed him that I would give him Na'im Akbar's book, *Breaking the Chains of Psychological Slavery*, and additional books that would assist him in achieving his goals. I encouraged him to embrace the belief that the Creator provided him with the capacity and ability to be all that he wanted to be, but he would have to expose his mind to the right information to achieve and maintain the desired results. On my departure from this particular correctional facility, the inmate stopped me and said, "Thanks! I needed that!" We then talked for another twenty minutes and embraced in the brother-to-brother handshake.

This inmate reminds me of many men I have worked with in my twenty-seven years of corrections and related experience. Corrections personnel are often presented with opportune moments to help an offender to pause, or as Kunjufu says, "Park right here for a moment," to assess and reflect on where they are in life.[4] Through the strength-based empowerment model, the African American male offender has the opportunity, the environment, and the incentive to participate in the process of reclaiming his spirit, mind, and body by employing them in meaningful, productive, healthy, and positive activities that replicate continual success until it becomes a habitual way of life.

Strength-based empowerment programming is cost effective and outcome driven. At the Fourth Annual White Privilege Conference (April 11, 2003) in Pella, Iowa, Jawanza Kujufu proclaimed that one in three African American males will be incarcerated by 2010. Our program allows leaders to effectively address the causes that perpetuate the staggering incarceration of African American males. Incorporating our theory into treatment programs enables government agencies responsible for the custody and care of African American males to effectively, efficiently, and permanently end the failures of our correctional facilities.

Our strength-based empowerment theory provides positive change and results. In his book, *State of Emergency: We Must Save African American Males*, Kunfuju attests that African American males thrive in nurturing environments that are filled with role models and positive peer pressure.[5] These elements are an integral part of the strength-based empowerment theory.

In writing this book, I am reminded of an inmate who said to me in a parole commission interview, "Don't take the hope out of my world." He was an older African American male who was considered an elder among the African American offenders. This book is an attempt to recognize, validate, and promote the hope that exists in every correctional staff member and offender. It is built and stands upon the motto: "I will achieve. You will achieve. We will achieve."

ACKNOWLEDGEMENTS

I thank with all my heart, mind, and soul, my wife and co-author of this book, Kimm Hurley-Smith, for her inspiration, support, and understanding; for believing in me, for her patience with my challenging behavior, and most of all for her contributions to this book. Without her encouragement, co-authorship, and dedication to our marriage, this book would not be a reality.

I am compelled to thank my family members; my children (JJ, Kizzy, Leonard and Justin), mother and father (Valerie and Jerry, Sr.), grandchildren (Justyce, Elijah, Isaiah and Journey), sisters (Nancy and Valerie) and brothers (David, Walter and Michael), sister-in-laws, brother-in-laws, aunts, uncles, nephews, and nieces for their unwavering support.

I also want to recognize the following individuals for their support, encouragement, and love: my mentors, Mr. Glenn Perkins and Mr. Ralph Jefferson.

I thank the gods of my ancestors and the Creator for their love, blessings, and protection.

INTRODUCTION

The goals of the strength-based empowerment model are:

To improve the level of safety in correctional or other confinement facilities through offenders' participation in African-centered empowerment groups

To provide effective African-centered strategies for reducing prison violence and inappropriate conduct

To increase offenders' participation in treatment programs

To provide correctional and law enforcement personnel an approach that can result in a positive, productive, and continual life change in African American male offenders

To help African American offenders make productive use of their time for success when they increase their potential to reenter society

To provide a healthy, supportive, culturally responsive, and effective program for Lifting the Spirit, Reprogramming the Mind, Instilling Self-Love, and Developing Self-Reliance in African American Male Offenders.

The number one goal of any confinement facility is safety and providing that safety efficiently and reliably. To achieve effective and consistent compliance from an offender, the correctional staff would be most effective if the offender is convinced that it is in his best interest to be positive. The primitive response to a hostile environment begs for safety from all participants. The offender wants to be safe as much as the correctional staff. Helping them to see their common goal is vital to reaching it. Once the common goal is understood compliance can occur.

The strength-based empowerment theory provides a framework offenders can commit to whereby they develop the level of motivation needed to maintain positive behavior. Amos N. Wilson indicates that true psychological and social sanity is obtained through self-knowledge and self-awareness. Self-knowledge and self-awareness are at the foundations of the strength-based empowerment model.

Our model recognizes that all people have strengths that can be identified, utilized, and magnified in their minds, bodies, and souls. A strengthening process is needed to build the capacity within individuals to maximize their potential, while minimizing their negative thoughts and habits and applying their decision-making and thought processes responsibly and consistently. This process enables correctional and related professionals to efficiently and effectively contribute to the person's positive self-actualization of responsible behavior, healthy decision-making and self-motivated stewardship of his life goals and daily agenda.

Budgetary challenges at all levels of American government have again required politicians, criminal justice and correctional officials, and taxpayers to re-examine the trends in criminal justice, offender management, recidivism, and public safety. The treatment programming, criminal laws, and governmental policies, procedures and practices have presented dismal results of historical incarceration and unacceptable recidivism and costs. These efforts have threatened the stability and capabilities of the educational systems at K–12 through college level all across America.

The strength-based empowerment model provides all interested parties an opportunity for remarkable improvement in rehabilitation and recidivism. Keep in mind, offenders also want to end their entanglement with the nefarious cycle of crime. Our model connects offenders, criminal justice and correctional officials, families, and communities in a positive alliance.

In the early 1990s, I met with a repeat offender who had recently completed the alcohol and other drug treatment program. I was concluding a parole interview when he reluctantly and apprehensively asked if he could speak to me about a group of African male offenders who had been meeting to support each other. He asked me if I would be willing to come to the group to speak about how to shape a positive life. He indicated that though they had been meeting, they did not know how to proceed with the group.

This inmate thought I could provide some wisdom, direction, and motivation for the group. I asked him why he wanted me to talk with them. He said that he had heard about me through other inmates as being "all right." Therefore, he felt I possessed some things they were looking for and needed to turn their lives around. I asked him for some time to think about his request. Before I responded to the request to speak to the group, he and other members of their group again asked me to come and talk with them, so I agreed.

The interaction with the group gave me an opportunity to experience sharing, learning, role modeling, nurturing, support, and guidance on an entirely new level.

As an African American male weaned on the civil rights movement, I have an enormous passion and commitment to improve the quality of life of African people and the disenfranchised. My connection with this support group for African American male offenders with life challenging issues of substance abuse, domestic violence, manhood, intimacy, anger, fatalism, limited marketable skills, and emotional instability gave me the opportunity to apply my service and commitment in a new dimension.

I believe the Creator offered me this opportunity to redirect my efforts toward fashioning a better world for African Americans. I was able to channel my efforts to individuals and away from a system that asserted discouragement, dehumanization, and degradation for African Americans. The chance to equip individual African American males with the knowledge and tools to be positive, productive, and contributing members of society provided great appeal and motivation for me to participate in this venture.

It seemed that the system only provided a modicum of progress, many times illusionary and temporary. In the same manner that the old folks would say, "If you get an education, they cannot take it away from you," I saw this as an opportunity to give these men a gift to help them navigate and negotiate their environment effectively.

In 1991, the initial group started with seven African American male offenders who had completed Alcohol and Other Drug Abuse (AODA) treatment at the largest minimum facility in the Wisconsin Prison System. Their

AODA instructor pulled the group together because he realized that if African American graduates were to have any chance of successfully reintegrating into their communities and families, they needed more than what the generic AODA treatment provided. This instructor, Mr. Ray Coleman, used the Circle of Recovery effort started by Kenny Hall in California, which he had learned of from a television documentary conducted by Bill Moyers.

I provided the group structure, guidance, life skills, and African-centered programming, making Coleman's initial effort a reality and applicable to the African American experience. Working from the premise that "self-knowledge is the key to mental health," I discovered that my primary points should be **self-knowledge, success, accountability, self-empowerment, self-love, self-determination,** and **collectivity of purpose.** I also provided some insight on living a responsible life, being a responsible man, citizen, parent, and partner from an Afro-centric perspective.

I shared a passage with the group from *Mis-education of the Negro*, by Carter G. Woodson, 1993.[6] The passage reads:

When you control a man's thinking you do not have to worry about his actions. You do not have to tell him not to stand here or go yonder. He will find his "proper place" and will stay in it. You do not need to send him to the back door. He will go without being told. In fact, if there is no back door, he will cut one for his special benefit. His education makes it necessary.

I have used this passage from the "Father of Black History" as the idiom that symbolizes our theory's rationale for **Circle of Empowerment Groups** and the cultural specific **LINKS of Empowerment.** It sadly applies even more in the twenty-first century as substantiated by the overrepresentation of African American males in prison, in special education classes, in the ranks of the unemployed, and in the growing rate of high school dropouts.

The Circle Group evolved from these early beginnings and experiences. The initial group existed for two years with as many as fifty inmates participating in the group sessions. I conducted the groups as my work schedule permitted.

It was not my goal to expand the groups. The success of the offenders in the group generated its expansion. The offenders in the initial group and the promotion of the program at other institutions formed the basis for requests from wardens and superintendents to start a group in their particular facilities. Correctional administrators/leaders wanted the Circle Groups for the following purposes:

(1) To provide a safe environment (2) To provide a program that enhanced (3) partnership between staff and offenders (4) To provide offenders a positive alternative for development and devotion of time and effort (5) To provide offenders an experience to influence their minds and actions toward positive results.

Due to this overwhelming interest from correctional administrators, staff, and offenders, I began establishing other groups, primarily at minimum correctional facilities. Volunteers staffed the program. There was no budget, which required that I personally purchase books and other materials. The administration of each facility obtained staff or an outside volunteer to conduct the group. I started the groups and trained the volunteers to conduct the group.

During this time, I also published a monthly newsletter that contained the writings of Circle members and information on the groups. This excerpt is taken from the February 2001, Volume 2, Issue 2 of the Jackson Correctional Institution Circle of Recovery/Renewal Newsletter:

The Circle of Recovery is like a big "Circle of Support." If you are new to prison, it can help you through where others have already been. If you have been looking for something to pass time, it's the Circle of Recovery that can take up a little time. If you are being released soon, or maybe transferred, then the Circle can be a link to resources to help you. It will make you think, laugh, and give you support and resources.

While there were no funds to collect data on the success of the offenders, I received anecdotal information. The requests from correctional personnel and offenders clearly validated the value and interest in the program. Both correctional staff and offenders indicated an improvement in the relationship between officers and inmates. There appeared to be fewer conduct reports. Inmate participation in treatment programs increased. Inmates increased their participation in self-help activities, for example making teddy bears for abused children, repairing eyeglasses for the low income, and inmate study groups. Inmates indicated that they looked forward to the weekly group meetings. It provided them an opportunity to reveal their achievements, frustrations, and goals in a nurturing and trusting environment.

As of 2008 the initial groups still exist in the Wisconsin Prison System. The groups continue to be conducted by volunteers. The interest and need for the groups still exist. Correctional administration is supporting the groups and offenders are attending.

PART 1

THE PHILOSOPHY

AFRICAN AMERICANS IN PRISON

The *Covenant with Black America* published in 2006 provides the following stark and reverberating statistics on the incarceration, arrests and conviction of African American males, females and youth:

Of the 2.1 million inmates today, 910,000 are African American. Blacks make up 43.9 percent of the state and federal prison populations but only 12.3 percent of the U.S. population. Whites account for 69 percent of the U.S. population and 34.7 percent of those incarcerated.

One out of every three black males born today can expect to go to prison. 1.4 million African American men, or 13 percent, have currently or permanently lost their right to vote as a result of a felony conviction—seven times the national average.

African Americans constitute 13 percent of all monthly drug users, but they represent 35 percent of arrests for drug possession, 55 percent of convictions, and 74 percent of prison sentences.

On any given day, one of every fourteen black children has a parent in prison.

One in every eighteen black women born today can expect to go to jail in her lifetime; this is six times the rate for white women.

Black women born today are five times more likely to go to prison in their lifetimes than black women born in 1974.

While African Americans represent 15 percent of those below the age of eighteen, they are 26 percent of all youths arrested, 46 percent of those detained in juvenile jails, and 58 percent of all juveniles sent to adult prison.

Nationwide, young black offenders are more than twice as likely to be transferred to adult court as their white counterparts. [7]

These statistics invite all of us to analyze the impact of these numbers on the African American family. Many African Americans have a close family member who has been or is currently in jail or prison. The added responsibility of having an incarcerated family member and its psychological effect has continued to burden these families in a variety of ways. When more than 910,000 African American men are in prison the results are: mothers are without the support of their sons, children are without the guidance and love of their fathers, wives/girlfriends are abandoned and left to fend for themselves; in a society that is less kind to single women.

Data about the types of crimes that African American males commit clearly speak to the emotional numbness they experience in response to living in a hostile environment. It is much easier for African American males to get their hands on drugs to sell in their communities than it is for them be offered jobs or training opportunities. Ironically taxpayers support the confinement of men who might benefit more from learning about themselves and learning to live and work responsibly so that they are in a position to support and contribute to society in positive ways.

The strength-based empowerment theory is designed to address the social and emotional issues unique to African American offenders, so that upon their release they can live a crime-free life and be productive members of society. Our theory recognizes that the incarceration of a person is usually the result of a trauma. The person has experienced hopelessness, powerlessness, and fatalism. The loss of freedom normally requires an action of devastating proportions. Opting into an environment that subjugates a person is generally precipitated by overwhelming circumstances.

In most cases, the road to confinement and subjugation begins in the early years. The mindset to create a hopeless, powerless, and fatalistic person takes many negative, degrading, and dehumanizing experiences to amass a self-destructive, disconnected, disoriented, and discouraged individual. All individuals are products of their environment, and if the environment offers experiences that erode the person's self-confidence and hope, the society is communicating to these people that they are disposable.

A person who does not see him or herself as a full and participating member of a group or society is more than likely not to act in the interest of that group or society. The strength-based empowerment theory helps the African American male find productive, positive, and rewarding ways to connect and become an active participant in the dominant society that he feels has an aversion to his existence and survival. Using historical examples of overcoming obstacles can connect African American prisoners to themselves in a productive manner, while offering them the opportunity to examine thoughts that prevent them from productive behaviors.

HITS OF DESTRUCTION

Traditional western psychological theories do not take into account the estimated ten to twenty-five million Africans who died on slave ships on the journey from Africa to the Americas. The impact of this crime against humanity, its aftermath of racism, and the psychological ramifications of slavery on the overall wellbeing of African Americans have largely been ignored. Understanding the repercussions of the numerous psychological hits of destruction that African Americans must negotiate each day is essential in the development of programs which speak to their experience. Understanding their attempts to retain self-respect is additionally essential to the development of effective programming. A process with the aim to speak to the resulting mixture of self-hatred and societal contempt. "Noting that mainstream theoretical perspectives often ignore race, racism and structural relations..."[8]

Many statistics demonstrate the effects these hits of destruction have upon African Americans. For the 15.5 million African American males living in the United States today, life expectancy is 62.9 years compared to 68.9 for white men. Infant mortality is 27.6 per 1,000 for African Americans compared to 14.1 for whites, and black male infant morality exceeds that of black females. The outpatient admission rate to mental health clinics and psychiatric hospitals is 998 per 100,000 for African Americans males; for white males it's 642 per 100,000. Inpatient admission rates are 873.4 per 100,000 for black males, compared to 599.4 per 100,000 for whites.[9]

As we can see, the African American male in the United States is still involved in numerous "firsts," as Haki R. Madhubuti so eloquently states in his book, *Black Men, Obsolete, Single and Dangerous*: "...the first jailed, first killed in the streets, first unemployed, first fired, first confined to mental institutions, first imprisoned, first lynched, first involved with drugs and alcohol, first miseducated, first denied medical treatment, first suicide, first to be divorced, first denied the normal benefits of this country, first to be blamed for all black problems, indeed black men are the first when it comes to being victims.[10]

Our theory's **LINKS of Empowerment,** which is discussed in detail in Part Three, is the center of our strength-based program. The following illustration displays how the LINKS (Safety, Belonging, Spirituality, and Positive Outcomes) shield the African American male from the environmental issues he negotiates on a daily basis. It shows the LINKS residing in the knowledge base, operations, and performance of the mind. From the illustration, the reader is provided a picture of the numerous hits African American males may encounter on a daily basis. It also defines the hits that deplete, derail, and distract them from obtaining healthy, productive, and positive growth. With the LINKS, the African American male's protective and regenerating layers deflect these hits from penetrating and incapacitating his mind, body, and soul.

This illustration communicates that the strength-based empowerment theory focuses on the offender's thoughts to produce true positive transformation. Our approach grounds the person in the belief that their thoughts and higher levels of consciousness are the keys to their success. It promotes the theme, "If you can believe it, you can conceive it." Carter G. Woodson, Mis-education of the Negro, 1993

HITS OF DEPLETION DERAILMENT/ DESTRUCTION

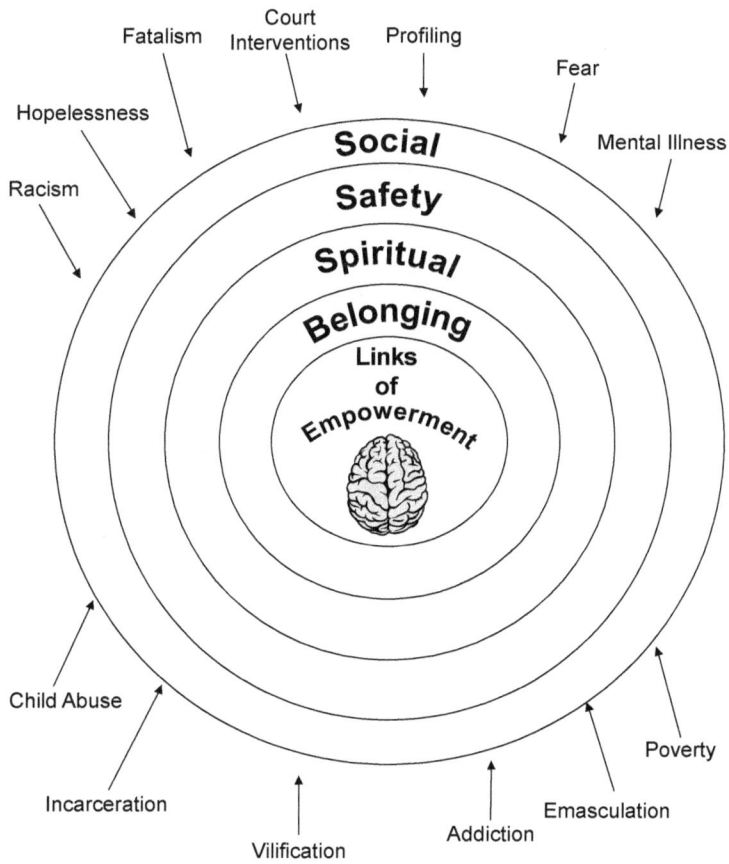

PHILOSOPHY

From 1980 to 1996, the suicide rate more than doubled among black males from fifteen to nineteen years of age. Experimenting with drugs and alcohol at an early age, undiagnosed mental health problems, trouble with the law, family isolation and a deep resentment for white society that looks like self-loathing seems to be the story. The cycle of criminal behavior and self-loathing could have been the factor for thinking that suicide was a better alternative. As we examine the thoughts of individuals who believe they are a victim, we realize that the terror they cause themselves is usually greater than what was done to them. It is common knowledge that many African Americans are criticized for being angry; this anger lives on the inside of their thoughts and is played out in behavioral choices against themselves. Many young men determine very young that their life is worth putting on the line in the name of respect, regardless of who they encounter including the police. When a person sees the world as a hostile place, they live in it as if their existence is always threaten. The thoughts that shackle the mind from the past remain chained to the African American male offender. His irrational acts to escape the harshness of life are apparent. Some of these thoughts include I am powerless, no one cares about me, I'll take what I want and nobody will step on me. Some of them turn against themselves by committing suicide.

The mental health system has developed a poor understanding of anger and spends much of its time scared of facing the anger that is presented in their offices. There is usually a policy that pertains to "irate" patients and it rarely includes treatment. "Irate" patients are removed from the setting as quick as possible with the assistance of the police. On the other hand anger is a legitimate emotion that needs examining. Anger gets fueled by the responses to it and therefore goes untreated. I remember working in a mental health setting where any angry African American client was referred to me. It took me awhile to understand the unwritten policy before I became angry myself. Many of the patients suffered from severe clinical depression and others were suicidal. Depression in the eyes of many clinicians look like a quiet person who is not eating, over sleeping, isolated or unable to perform ordinary tasks. Other severe symptoms such as persistent anger, engaging in self-destructive behavior, or challenging the police are overlooked because the patient is never examined. This speaks volumes for the treatment of African Americans in public mental health settings.

Questions related to firearms in the home should be asked on a regular basis. The clinician must be aware of the methods and symptoms that African Americans present in order to complete a thorough examination. If the clinician is untrained in the history of the culture and unaware of how depression manifests itself, the patient will go untreated. Many patients have a long history of mistrust and are unwilling to join with a therapist until they have developed some sense of commitment to each other. This can be the vital link to services for clients who are seen as resistant to treatment. Sometimes the person doesn't want to start a relationship with someone that they think does not understand them and therefore will request an African American. Or on the other hand request someone who will not judge me and has had similar experiences. One thing for sure, all of the stories of self-hatred are the same. There are no new stories, only recycled old ones.

African Americans could be resistant to medication, hospitalization, and treatment based on stories that run nonstop in their heads, yet these stories like all stories must be examined so that the terror they produced can be eliminated. There are many stories that contribute to suicidal ideation. The minds of African American males are filled with stories of hopelessness, absence of love, pain, invalidation, fear and vilification. These stories contain truths and untruths.

There are some stereotypes that encourage African Americans to be strong no matter the circumstances; this denies the human qualities that all others have when it comes to an array of emotions. If crying is seen as weak or deficient, a person is left with expressing their sadness in other ways, which symbolize "I am strong". This expression can be misunderstood and cause communication problems.

The LINKS enable the offender to reconstruct his thinking so that he can make better decisions about himself. He begins to speak with confidence, clarity, compassion, and commitment. He sees the truth as an ally. He does not waiver in untruths. He articulates his ideas with precision. His conversation is reality-based and practical. His perspective is mature. He recognizes his limitations and accepts the awesome challenge of his goals. He is open to advice and rejects the propaganda of failure and exploitation. He attaches to things that reinforce his development and growth. He avoids poisonous words, adverse incidents, and thoughts that attack his new and positive foundation. He recognizes the negativity that is transmitted through carriers of contempt, jealousy, fear, racism, and dominance. He minimizes the influence of the doubtful. He prohibits the doubtful from depositing their heinous program. He sees the universe as friendly.

The LINKS encourage the offender to do the following:
Rally around African-Centered knowledge
Rally around spirituality
Rally around the collective – We are, therefore; I am!
Rally around love and self-acceptance
Rally around achievement
Rally around hope
Rally around goals
Rally around reality in thought
Rally around questioning untruths

THE PREMISES OF THE PHILOSOPHY

The strength-based empowerment philosophy consists of several premises. Our first premise involves the concept that gaining a deeper understanding must be done in the context of one's **collective history.** This embraces culturally specific treatment.

As with any culture, members of an ethnic group often share certain beliefs, values, habits, customs, and norms. Ethnic groups define themselves differently because of special cultural features. These distinctions may arise from language, religion, historical experiences, and geographic location. Additional distinguishing features include a collective name, belief in common descent, a sense of solidarity, and an association with a specific country.

Black on Black Violence—The Psychodynamics of Black-Annihilation in Service of White Domination, by Amos N. Wilson, supports our theory's premise regarding the need for understanding the collective history: "...his criminal identity must be exorcised and a new, authentic one constructed through a new infusion of Afrocentric information, supportive social interactions, and the development of new competencies and associations.[11]

When the African American offender learns about his history, he develops a greater sense of himself. He is encouraged to take responsibility for his decisions, because it becomes part of his collective responsibility. This collective responsibility enables him to maximize the present by using his time in prison to prepare to be a better family and community member.

Further, knowing one's history helps individuals gain insight and understanding of cultural strengths, provides hope and determination for the future, helps to successfully negotiate the challenges of life, and also helps gain a better understanding of relationships with others.

His true sense of self is partially developed through learning about the unique history of African Americans, including not only slavery and internalized racism but also about the our connection to the history of Africa. It is through this sense of self that we achieve our greatest potential.

A second premise of our program philosophy is the emphasis on encouraging the African American male to recognize, reveal, and redress his thoughts that create **emotional pain**. Many African American prisoners have emotional issues that go unidentified in the traditional treatment process. This emotional pain drives their decision-making process. Beliefs in untrue thoughts promote self-destructive behavior, errors in thinking, and poor judgment. These poor decisions support the recapitulation of painful experiences. Western psychology, which for the most part is standardized on white males, has yet to prove its validity on the white population. It is clear that it has little to no effect on the African American populations, in prison or otherwise based on the statistics presented earlier.

The *individualism* for which many of the Western theories were developed goes against the collective culture and spirit of Africans, and therefore, African Americans. The individualism that attempts to help individuals differentiate produces resistance from those of African descent. The African American culture considers working in unison for the greater good as a core concept and regards individualism as detractive. The objective is to rise above one's own needs to meet the needs of the family and community. This concept of obligation to a greater purpose has given the African American assurance of survival.

Too often, the court system considers the African American offender's unwillingness to attend or participate in mandated therapy as an indication of not wanting to correct what has been defined as "antisocial behavior." Based on their misunderstanding of their own thoughts, many professionals who evaluate these men will only contribute more information to their files that supports further incarceration and misunderstanding.

Information about the African American experience in America and Africans in the world has not been institutionalized for students pursuing counseling degrees at institutions of higher learning. Therefore, we can assume that most of the professionals from these institutions, though probably unintentionally, would make inadequate diagnoses and recommendations regarding this population. To further complicate this issue, many African American prisoners who have no confidence in traditional therapy have learned to use therapy as a strategy to gain freedom, rather than as a pathway to develop strengths that would keep them out of jail and prison.

Emotionally, African Americans are dealing with layers and generations of self-hate and self-rejection that make it hard for them to achieve a healthy sense of self. Power and authority issues are played out in society. A demonstration of I am in control is very influential in the African American male. I am not in control is considered weak. When you are considered weak you are not safe and anyone can and will harm you, is the belief. Personal safety is vital in anyone's life. This is a major contributing factor to prison violence and violence in African American communities.

When a person has limited control over his life, he might attempt to gain control in unhealthy ways. However, with information that grounds the offender in who he is historically and culturally, he now has a foundation that provides a connection to emotional maturity. This creates space for spirituality, a higher sense of self, and an internal resistance to immature behaviors.

The strength-based empowerment theory recognizes that no one has the goal of subjugation to a life of pain, despair, disappointment, anger, hopelessness, loss of freedom, dereliction, and dysfunction. It acknowledges that the events in life such as racism, poverty, and family violence can become so overpowering that survival requires maladaptive coping mechanisms.

These maladaptive coping strategies support poor decision-making that can result in confinement and/or other retributions of society, such as being unemployed, uneducated, uninsured, and unreachable. The strength-based empowerment theory acknowledges that every person has the capability for self-love, self-respect, and self-determination, no matter what mistakes they have made in the past. It sees mistakes as gifts of self-knowledge.

This philosophy enables the African American male to rid himself of the caustic and debilitating elements that have infiltrated his mind, captured his soul, and smothered his spirituality. He develops a desire and commitment to be accountable.

The program philosophy also embraces the following themes:

■ Strength-Based = Identification of Strengths to Reinforce Hope

To achieve a positive lifestyle, a person must be seen through their strengths. A person's strengths serve as the nucleus of the rebuilding process. The development of the offender's strengths will enable him to minimize or eliminate his weaknesses, including the attraction to negativity, self-destruction, or hopelessness.

The LINKS and Circles are completely positive. In the Circle meeting, the men talk first about any achievement they had during the week. It might be not getting a major ticket or getting their GED or helping another inmate or dissociating from old friends or contacting an estranged parent to develop a relationship, or demonstrating forgiveness. The process reinforces itself over time.

■ History = Connecting the Men to Their Past in a Positive Manner

The infusion of history into a person's consciousness connects him to his spirit and identity. We believe that there is Spirit in everything and everything is Spirit. History provides the individual with the blueprints of successful ancestors whom they can emulate. As professed by Amos N. Wilson, it provides individuals with a strong foundation by shaping and transforming their personality.[12]

■ Belonging = Acknowledgement of Collective Responsibility

A sense of belonging is vital to a person's existence. It underpins their spirit, mind, and body. Through a sense of belonging, individuals can connect to something greater than themselves. This influences how they interact with others and their environment. Belonging to the collective helps people interpret, manage, and respond to the various challenges they encounter in life. This helps the men realize that their behavior effects more than themselves.

■ African-Centered Knowledge = Honoring Oneself

African-centered knowledge is critical to African Americans maximizing their full potential. This knowledge speaks to generations of achievements that a person can be proud of and connected to. It provides the informational reservoir for people to transform themselves into the most powerful human beings possible.

■ Achievement = Building Successes

Achievement is as integral to a person's self-esteem as oxygen is to blood. In our strength-based empowerment model, participants are offered numerous opportunities for achievement as well as recognition for their efforts.

■ Building Successes = Winning Attitude

Each success is a building block for improving the person's spirit, self-esteem, and motivation. As each concept builds upon the other the individual trains his mind to interpret situations differently. The result is a healthy perspective and positive responses.

■ Confidence and Self-motivation = Receptivity to Growing and Learning

The more solid a person's sense of self, the more inclined they are to experience new and challenging things that offer the opportunity for growth and success. They become more receptive to new ideas and concepts.

■ Education = Self-awareness and Preparedness

As a person's self-knowledge increases, so does his capacity for handling life. This greater capacity produces peace of mind and balance between the spirit, mind, and body. Knowledge of self clarifies a person's relationship to others, his environment, and his spiritual path in life.

■ Intention = Positive Outcomes

Individuals must develop a respectful understanding and appreciation of another person's position and intentions.

The appreciation of others serves to develop a witness and listener. As a listener one can learn and be present for others and themselves.

■ Safety = Stability

Safety is a mental phenomenon that manifests itself in behavior. It takes a sound mind and healthy thoughts, and consequently, stable behavior for an individual to hold his own safety and the safety of others in high regard. If a person is secure mentally and is spiritually grounded, then he can manifest safety spiritually and physically. Safety is developed from thinking and believing the thought I am safe. This can be achieved by knowing you are more than a body but a spirit that never dies.

■ Control = Commitment

Self-control is a reflection of the person's commitment to himself, his family, and his community. A person who has self-control understands how important it is to listen, to be a part of the collective, to be in balance, and to have integrity in the eyes of others. Commitment is saying what you mean and following through.

■ New Ideas = Maturity

When one has matured—like the old oak—through true and time-tested challenges, then his ideas are grounded deep like the roots of the oak, and can weather all. Ideas, therefore, spring forth with all options explored, with flexibility to incorporate concepts of similar purpose and usefulness.

PART 2

AFRICAN-CENTERED TREATMENT

AFRICAN-CENTERED
TREATMENT

The strength-based empowerment theory's African-centered models and values diversity by tailoring treatment to the specific target group. The approach is holistic. Thinking aloud to eliminate cognitive errors, encouraging, and confronting are built into the treatment program.

Our theory recognizes that a person is hampered in their quest for wholeness, self-actualization and denied their true destiny if they do not know the origin of their existence and the elements of their make-up. Dr. Na'im Akbar reminds us, "We must acquire consciousness of who we are and where we have been in order to operate to our full human capacity."[13]

In our program, the offender is acquainted and then thoroughly drenched in African and African American history. He is provided the full foundation of his existence, which originated in the motherland of Africa. Our model acknowledges that cultural connection and understanding are essential to the mental and physical health, stability, and capability of the African American male offender.

Here is a practical example: ignoring cultural connection and understanding is like not serving sweet potato pie and cornbread dressing on Thanksgiving. These different foods could also be alternated with the more traditional European dishes, or highlighted occasionally. When African American offenders think about or discuss Thanksgiving, these foods are most likely a part of the conversation. This provision indicates to the offender that the custodian recognizes the offender's uniqueness and preferences. It demonstrates an effort to connect with the offender in a positive way. It signals to the offender that the custodian sees him as a person of value. When value is acknowledged, it provides the seeds of harmony and appreciation.

Dr. Gloria Johnson Powell, Associate Dean for Faculty, University of Wisconsin Medical School, informed the participants at a conference titled *People with Mental Illness and Substance Abuse Issues in Criminal Justice: Promising Practices in Collaborative Interventions* that "difference does not mean deficit."[14] In an analogy using plants, she reminded us that certain plants need moist soil to exist and some plants thrive best in dry soil. Some plants require the sun to remain alive, while others can tolerate only moderate exposure to the sun and prefer that the majority of time be spent in the shade.

In our program, the offender is provided analogies like the plant analogy offered by Dr. Johnson Powell. This understanding of plant existence and survival helps the offender make a connection with his own existence, uniqueness, and requirements for survival. African American males need African-centered treatment and environments to thrive and survive the rigors of everyday life in a society that provides limited opportunities for their growth, development, and survival.

PROFESSIONAL PROFICIENCIES

In *Counseling Persons of African Descent,* Parham indicates that the African-centered paradigm requires the service professional to be proficient and to connect with the client in at least five areas to be maximally effective in healing the client:[15]

Spiritual realities
Cultural realities
Historical realities
Socio-cultural realities
Political and racial realities

Usually, traditional treatment programs are missing political and racial realities, but the strength-based empowerment theory understands these are critical aspects of the African American experience that demand thorough consideration, assessment, and solutions. It accepts the premise that for people of African descent in America, race is an inescapable force influencing their mental and physical health, spirit, and capabilities of effectively managing life.

All of these realities are captured in our LINKS of Empowerment, which is discussed in Part 3. The LINKS provide correctional staff at all levels with an effective strategy to assist African American male offenders in becoming self-controlled, self-sufficient, productive, and positive role models.

The LINKS offer more definitive elements of the realities that African Americans must navigate and negotiate and become proficient in managing, to develop healthy and sound minds, to be in harmony with environment, and to attain full spiritual development and mastery of their innate attributes.

Racism's existence and web of destruction, debilitation, and dehumanization is demystified by our strength-based empowerment theory. Our model utilizes the LINKS as tools to effectively minimize the adverse effects of racism by strengthening the individual to manage this potent and pervasive negativity.

THE GROUP PROCESS

The focus of the group is on responsibility and accountability for one's thoughts and behavior. The members learn how having power over thoughts, which drive behavior, as well as making wise choices, are the most powerful tools in their emotional arsenal. They learn about intentions. The strength-based group process encourages and helps each member define what "responsible" personally means to him.

For one individual this might mean that he will start taking his prison wages and applying them toward supporting his family, rather than on his personal needs like hair care or to personal addictions such as cigarettes, drugs, candy, or soda. Another member may have the goal of staying "out of the hole." This member will need to avoid potentially hazardous situations, including not associating with certain prisoners, and focusing his time, energy, and thoughts on the things that will lead him toward remaining free of segregation, conduct reports, and longer prison stays.

Intentions

Our premise is that intentions are powerful phenomena that determine the men's ability to achieve their expected outcomes. Each member must critically examine his own intentions to develop a healthy perspective and knowledge base in this powerful arena. In the group process, the men think aloud and openly examine their thoughts. The group provides feedback that identifies the intentions of these thoughts.

This process encourages trust and belonging in the group. The offender is educated on how to evaluate possible ramifications and to develop alternative solutions or paths toward his intended goal. The member's examination of his personal intentions is an effective intervention utilized within the group.

Confrontation

The intervention of confrontation enables the African American male offender to examine, in front of others, his thinking process for objective feedback. This intervention addresses the concept that a person often cannot see a clear picture of himself, while others can sometimes see what the individual cannot. After they have bonded, the men will take many risks in telling stories about their successes and failures.

Specific confrontation is a practice that the group uses to help its members acknowledge flawed thinking and behaviors. The members use "I" statements to respond to errors in thinking and behaviors, as well as ask questions to clarify statements. This process encourages the members to think through their decisions and entertain all possible consequences, and also promotes the replacement of short-term gains and immediate gratification with long-term opportunities and delayed gratification.

Many lessons are learned from these interactions. A collective sense of belonging and a common purpose provide the means by which the men can develop intimate relationships with their families and communities. The all-male group process assists members with support and encouragement from men with a variety of experiences and maturity levels. Group membership operates as a surrogate family, which is vital to the process. The older men become father, uncle, and grandfather figures, demanding the respect and responsibility of the African American tradition.

The strength-based empowerment theory's group process encourages many expectations of its members, including remaining open to new ideas/approaches, self-control, using good judgment, and seeking alternatives to resolutions. There is an acceptance that every person is a role model. These expectations serve as principles to guide their daily lives.

AFRICAN PRINCIPLES

Teaching African principles, which is an integral part of the strength-based empowerment theory, promotes empathy, ethics, and values in the members of the group. Our treatment groups are structured to reinforce the principle that all behavior is collective rather than individual, meaning that a person's behavior has an impact beyond himself. When the members realize that their behaviors are powerful and have an effect on many people, it creates group responsibility and teaches empathy. Additionally, the collective group is used to role model, and to reflect the challenges and strengths in a process that is holistic and culturally specific.

In our **Circle of Empowerment Groups,** the members interact with each other, expressing themselves in language that promotes understanding and validation. A developing sense of membership creates belonging, motivation, self-control, and responsibility.

MAAT
Many eminent African American psychologists including Wade Nobles, Maulana Korenga, Na'im Akbar, Thomas White, and Jawanza Kunjufu advance the principles of MAAT, which consist of seven virtues: righteousness, truth, justice, harmony, balance, reciprocity, and order. The ultimate aim of this traditional belief system of ancient Egypt (Kemet) is for a person to become "one with God" or to "become like God." It values life. MAAT maintains that

everything has a life force that contributes to the balance of nature and therefore must be respected.

To examine some of the traditions and rituals of the numerous African nations, which reflect MAAT and whose principles are incorporated in our theory, we can look to the Sudanese. Like other East African herders, the *Dinka*, a populous Nilotic (indigenous East African peoples originating in northeast Africa in the region of the Nile River) in southern Sudan, lives in symbiosis with their cattle. The Dinkas use the cattle's skin, milk, meat, blood, and waste products as part of their daily living.

Anthropologist Nadine Peacock studied the *Efe* people of Zaire. Peacock found that the Efe live in small mobile groups called "bands." These bands depend on each other for survival. They have a common purpose and goal in life.

Without the appropriate information, many would assume that women all over the African continent perform tasks similar to those prescribed by American culture. However, cross-cultural comparisons show that differences exist, many of which are based on cultural training, rather than biology. In Kenya, for example, the men do the laundry.

Another example of the MAAT tradition can be seen in the pastoral *Masai* of Kenya. All Masai males born during the same four-year period are circumcised together and belong to the same named group throughout their lives. The groups move through grades, of which the most important is the warrior grade.

Certain parts of East and Central Africa have pan-tribal councils that consist of secret societies of men and women. Similar to American college fraternities and sororities, these associations have secret initiation ceremonies. Among the *Mende* of Sierra Leone, the men and women belonging to these secret societies carry great influence. The male groups, the *Poro,* are responsible for training the boys in social conduct, ethics, religion, and political and economic activities. The leadership in this group oversees social control, management of disputes, and regulations.

There are numerous examples from African culture that support the strength-based empowerment theory's contention that African Americans excel in groups where there is trust, a common purpose, and clear expectations of its members. This concept is also applicable to gang activity.

AFRICAN-CENTERED PSYCHOLOGY

The strength-based empowerment model is specifically designed for African Americans who are not aligned or connected with their true self and spirit. It is grounded in African American traditions, values, and beliefs. It holds that African American individuals—who are slaves to criminality and susceptible to messages and images of destruction, illusion, and servitude to others—can best be reclaimed, renewed, and redirected with an African-centered model because, from a spiritual perspective, these individuals are African.

In *Counseling Persons of African Descent*, black psychologist Thomas A. Parham defines African-centered psychology as:[16]

The dynamic manifestation of the unifying African principles, values, and traditions. It is the self-conscious "centering" of psychological analysis and applications in African reality, culture, and epistemology. African-centered psychology examines the process that allows for the illumination and liberation of the spirit. Relying on the principles of harmony with the universe as a natural order of existence, African-centered psychology recognizes: the Spirit that permeates everything that is; the notion that everything in the universe is interconnected; the value that the collective is the most salient element of existence; and the idea that communal self-knowledge is the key to mental health.

CULTURAL IMPACT

As provided in *YURUGU: An African-Centered Critique of European Cultural Thought and Behavior* by Marimba Ani, Wade Nobles defines culture as "a process which gives peoples a general design for living, and patterns for interpreting their reality."[17] The strength-based empowerment theory incorporates African-centeredness and African culture as the framework for people of African descent to define and interpret their reality, self, and future.

Marimba Ani offers the following **characteristics of culture:**[18]

It acts to unify and to order experience, so that its members perceive organization, consistency, and system. In this respect, it provides a "worldview" that offers orienting conceptions of reality.

It gives people group identification, as it builds on shared historical experience, creating a sense of collective cultural identity.

It "tells" its members "what to do," thereby creating a "voice" of prescriptive authority.[19] To its members, culture represents values (which they themselves have created together out of shared experiences) as a systematic set of ideas and a single coherent statement.

It provides the basis for commitment, priority, and choice, thereby imparting direction to group development and behavior: indeed, it acts to limit the parameters of change and to pattern the behavior of its members.

In this way culture helps initiate and authorize its own creation.

It provides for the creation of shared symbols and meanings. It is, therefore, the primary creative force of collective consciousness, and it is that which makes it possible to construct a national consciousness.

For all the above reasons, it impacts on the definition of group interest and is potentially political.

AFROCENTRIC MODEL OF DEVELOPMENT

Many researchers have noted the failure of traditional treatment approaches to tap the underlying cultural processes and African worldview that guide the behavior of African American parents and their children. The strength-based empowerment theory's Afrocentric model of development recognizes these important underlying issues.

The African worldview includes numerous dimensions that reflect ways in which African American people may think, feel, and act. However, it should be noted that there are variations in the degree to which members of racial/ethnic groups adhere to the dimensions of their groups' worldview. Following are the African worldview dimensions from which our theory evolves:

Spirituality, or the belief in a Supreme Being, goes beyond religiosity by focusing on the qualities of people, rather than on material possessions.

Communalism, or interpersonal orientation, reflects an emphasis on group over individual, cooperation rather than competition, and people-focused versus task-focused.

Harmony refers to the importance of integrating one's life into a whole, recognizing one's interdependency with the environment, and seeking unity rather than control.

Expressive communication, or orality, emphasizes transmitting and receiving information orally, through rhythmic communication and "call and response."

Affective sensitivity provides emotional cues reflecting the integration of feelings and socialization of the verbal and the nonverbal (e.g., an expectation that a child will alter its behavior with a gesture or a look, a cultural survival socialization).

Rhythmic movement is expressed in gross motor behavior and reflects an interest in flexible, yet patterned action.

Multidimensional perception or verse is illustrated in the preference for stimulus variety in learning, with both parent and child valuing experimentation.

Stylistic expressiveness refers to the valuing of the individual's unique style, flair, or spontaneity in expressing oneself when it reflects group goals.

Time as a social phenomenon reflects the view that time is spiritual, not material or linear. An event starts when the first person arrives and ends when the last person leaves.

Positivity refers to the desire to see good in all situations, no matter how bad they seem to be on the surface.

Historically, research on African Americans in particular has shifted focus several times. The inferiority model has been used to describe cultural behaviors over time. Researchers have attempted to present models that consign African Americans as inferior to those of white European descent. Using a model of inferiority would explain all behaviors that were not appropriate according to the European worldview. This model was absent of the historical underpinnings of African culture and did not take into account many strengths of the African American male.

Amos N. Wilson provides the term "social amnesia" (originating with Russell Jacoby, *Social Amnesia*) for African Americans deprived of their African worldview and history.[20] He avows that a person with this burden lives by fear, anxiety, terror, and trauma. He contends that social amnesia causes many of the murders, deaths, and destruction in black communities.

Our model demonstrates to offenders that they are human beings with value. It respects the offender as a person with strengths. It focuses on the offender's humanity while guiding him to accept responsibility for his actions and accountability for his criminal behavior. It provides the inmate the opportunity to grow and develop as a responsible human being who is the captain of his destiny. African American heroes and heroines are provided as demonstrations of perseverance to succeed against huge odds.

CULTURAL UNITY

Cultural unity is an integral component of the strength-based empowerment theory. Boykins explains this concept as follows:[21]

Cultural unity expresses itself in the form of nine distinct but interrelated dimensions of African-American culture: (1) *spirituality,* an approach to life as being essentially vitalistic rather than mechanistic, with the conviction that nonmaterial forces influence people's everyday lives; (2) **harmony,** the notion that one's fate is interrelated with other elements in the scheme of things, so that humankind and nature are harmonically joined; (3) *movement,* an emphasis on the interweaving of movement, rhythm, percussiveness, music, and dance, which are taken as central to psychological health; (4) *verve,* a propensity for relatively high levels of stimulation, to action that is energetic and lively; (5) *affect,* an emphasis on emotions and feelings, together with a special sensitivity to emotional cues and a tendency to be emotionally expressive; (6) *communalism,* a commitment to social connectedness that includes an awareness that bonds and responsibilities transcend individual privileges; (7) *expressive individualism,* the cultivation of a distinctive personality and a proclivity for spontaneous, genuine personal expression; (8) *oral tradition,* a preference for oral/aural modes of communication in which oral virtuosity—the ability to use alliterative, metaphorically colorful, graphic forms of spoken language—is emphasized and cultivated; and (9) *social perspective,* an orientation in which time is treated as passing through a social space rather than a material one, in which time can be recurring, personal, and phenomenological."

ETHNICITY

Ethnicity is also important to the strength-based empowerment theory. The following list illustrates our view of ethnicity in regards to providing African-centered treatment for offenders. Ethnicity:

Determines what mental health is.
Determines the manifestation of symptoms.
Determines defensive styles.
Determines patterns of coping and anxiety.
Determines how fear, depression, guilt, anger get defined.
Determines how fear, guilt, and anger get reinforced.
Determines the help-seeking patterns.
Determines utilization of treatment.

Counselors and other psychological service providers need to recognize that as long as African Americans are subjected to racist and oppressive conditions in this society and are confronted with the question of how much to compromise their "Blackness" in order to successfully assimilate, they (blacks) will continue to need therapeutic assistance in struggling with issues of:[22]

■ _**Self-differentiation versus preoccupation with assimilation:**_ the dynamic in which an individual strives to become comfortable with the recognition that he or she is worthwhile human being regardless of valuation and validation from whites.

■ _**Body transcendence versus preoccupations with body image:**_ an individual strives to become comfortable with one's physical self, which may be characterized by a continuum of possibilities ranging from African to Afro-European characteristics (i.e., very dark vs. very light skin, very coarse vs. very straight hair, very thick vs. very thin lips).

■ *Ego-transcendence versus self-absorption:* person strives to become secure enough within himself so that he is able to develop personal ego strength by contributing to the uplifting of his people, rather than himself exclusively. Such efforts are consistent with the African worldview of "I am because we are, and because we are, therefore, I am."

Heppner and colleagues found that African American participants who were part of a culturally inclusive treatment program, for example, having an African American co-facilitator or inclusion of statistics and information related to the African American community, acknowledged that the treatment was more cognitively engaging than in a colorblind condition, in which race was never discussed.[23]

Many African Americans understand the extent to which members of the helping professions sometimes have functioned in an adversarial, competitive or an all-knowing posture, related to the treatment of African American inmates. The social workers for the most part discount the strengths of the inmates, because it ultimately supports their superior roles, and maintains the subservient and dependent position of the inmate.

In *Counseling Persons of African Descent*, researchers assert that it is difficult, if not impossible, to understand the lifestyles of African people using the traditional psychological theories that were developed by psychologists of European American descent.[24] The treatment programs have failed most inmates in general and more specifically African Americans.

Our strength-based empowerment theory acknowledges the unique plight of African American males' existence in American prisons and jails. We recognize how confinement directly affects their hopes, dreams, goals, family, and community by examining the rage, fear, and sadness that occurs within the African American male. African-centered treatment promotes healthy, productive recovery and renewal of the African American male during his incarceration and upon release.

PART 3

THE LINKS OF EMPOWERMENT

L = LIFE PROCESS

The LINKS of Empowerment is a lifelong process. It advises that adherence to the principles of self-empowerment be eternal. Like good habits, the LINKS refine the person's personality, increase the aptitude to effectively manage life's challenges, and improve decision-making and self-control for harnessing ultimate effectiveness.

I = INTELLECTUAL AWAKENING

The LINKS enable a person to tap into and release his innate abilities to increase knowledge, develop wisdom, and gain confidence in the pursuit, processing, and application of the information obtained.

N = NURTURING SELF

Through the LINKS, the person learns to appreciate and value himself. He acquires the knowledge to nurture himself and master techniques for personal growth and development.

K = KINSHIP

The LINKS help the offender connect to his African-centered ideology of kinship, in which the whole being is more important than the parts, as well as the importance of being in balance spiritually, mentally, and physically. Being trustworthy and honest is viewed as the individual's responsibility to himself and to the community.

S = SUPPORT

The LINKS are the support for the person's self-actualization, regeneration, and maintenance of his new reality. These tools of empowerment support the development of a sound, consistent, and persistent human spirit and force.

The strength-based empowerment theory's LINKS of Empowerment provide African American male offenders with the following:

(1) An educational pathway to understanding oneself
(2) An evaluation of thinking patterns that gives definition to behavior
(3) A sense of belonging and connectedness to oneself and the community
(4) A vision of hope for the future

Strengthening African American offenders by helping them become individuals who embrace and demonstrate a crime-free lifestyle, self-love, caring, support, self-control, good decision-making, self-sufficiency, and accountability is the cornerstone of the LINKS. Our ultimate goal is to help offenders achieve their optimum levels of self-empowerment. This attainment of self-empowerment enables the offender to achieve self-awareness, emotional development, stability, spiritual satisfaction, and preparedness to maximize opportunities in life.

METHODOLOGY

The LINKS combine to eliminate the excuses the offender has amassed to conceal his pain, frustration, hopelessness, fatalism, anger, and destructive tendencies. The LINKS enable the offender to identify the excuses that allow him to be irresponsible, unpredictable, selfish, a failure, a victim, fatalistic, hopeless, and to make poor choices, jeopardize progress, act on anger, embellish disappointment, and magnify unfairness.

Learning to deal with anger, frustration, and pain is a priority for offenders participating in the program. These three emotions trigger many of the poor decisions offenders make in the heat of the moment. As Amos N. Wilson substantiates in *The Falsification of African Consciousness*, a person must be out of his mind and remain out of his mind to continue behaving irresponsibly and destructively.[25] The LINKS help offenders to cleanse their minds and souls of negativity, which enables them to attain higher levels of emotional and spiritual growth.

The LINKS stress the essential dignity and individuality of developing male minds by helping them identify the good in themselves. When individuals are constantly perceived as worthless, it gives them permission to act those feelings out. By seeing the good in themselves, these men have a strong foundation from which to build self-preservation.

The LINKS of Empowerment uncover the hidden strengths of African American offenders by guiding them in answering the following questions:

How can I accept myself in this very moment?
How do I become what I want and need to be?
How do I maintain who I need to be for myself, my loved ones, and my community?

Many people in prison suffer from a variety of negative socio-environmental factors. They may have been raised in poor communities that had poor schools. They may have witnessed violence at a young age. They may have parents who suffered with drug and alcohol abuse. These socio-environmental factors affect children's innate physical and mental capabilities. Environment contributes in a mighty way to personality development.

Gunnings and Simkin propose that social, political, and economic factors that negatively affect the lives of African American clients must become the focus of more systemically oriented counseling practices.[26] If one is placed in an environment that manifests itself in negativity, then negative personality traits will evolve. One major trauma can cause a person to have hopeless thinking and increase both suicidal and homicidal thoughts. Numerous traumas which include dehumanizing, instillation of fear, power and control in an abusive manner can set up a predisposition for criminal and rebellious behavior.

When the essential stimuli for balanced self-awareness, positive spirituality, and healthy emotional development are absent, maladjustment can occur. Once a person formulates a criminal perspective on how to survive in the world and that perspective is reinforced through the environment, it can become second nature to commit acts for immediate self-satisfaction. This maladapted personality generates abnormal feelings, perceptions, and behaviors. These initial characteristics become habits over time and eventually become a way of life with their own standards of operation, which come into conflict with the code of behavior accepted in general society.

The recurring pain, disappointments, and harsh consequences are not severe enough to convince the offender to abandon his only power, belonging, value, and survival. No matter how hard he tries, he ends up serving the immediate self-gratification of criminal activity that possesses his mind, spirit, and soul.

In answering the question, "How did I become who I am?" the offender may move forward, but is overburdened by personal tragedies and daily reminders of his second-class citizenship, which illustrate lack of opportunities, constant occurrences of emasculation, and vile portrayals.

The conventional modalities of cognitive therapy and religion have marginal success for the African American male offender. Traditional European-based treatment or programming cannot balance the pain of disappointments, frustrations, emasculation, and fatalism he feels deep inside his body, soul, and spirit.

The LINKS of Empowerment provide the African American male offender with the ingredients to eliminate the shackles that enslave and consume his mind. The LINKS enable the offender to build his internal well of strength. They equip him with culturally specific information, strategies, and techniques that enable him to effectively and independently manage his environment and shield him against distractions and illusions of fatal thinking that haunt his existence.

How do I become what I want and need to be?

We teach that self-awareness is the first step. If you do not know where you came from, you will not know where your future lies. African and African American history, a central part of the curriculum, is consistently presented in every session.

African American culture has a strong oral tradition, whereas the dominant culture is oriented toward a written tradition. The LINKS use oral traditions to tell stories about history and life experiences that support and relate to the struggles these men negotiate in their lives on a daily basis during their incarceration.

Inmates often marvel with excitement and energy over the new knowledge of who they are. They connect in a real way with this illustrious history. The richness gives them pride. The tragedies and the less–than-admirable parts give them balance in maintaining a healthy perspective of the realities of life.

The offender learns to start "his"-story in African civilizations that set the foundation for the Romans, Greeks, and other civilizations that followed. Mindfully, the program does not begin with an examination of African American history. If treatment began with the American history of slavery, then the offender would start out from a perspective that the African American male is less than human and less than a man and, therefore, the ultimate minority.

In *The Psychology of Blacks: An African-Centered Perspective,* Cross, Parham, and Helms assert that for African Americans, identity serves three functions: (1) it provides a social anchor and meaning to one's existence; (2) it serves as a connection to the broader African community across the globe; and (3) it serves as a protection or buffer against the social forces that continually bombard the psyche with non-affirming and, in some cases, dehumanizing messages.[27]

The majority culture provides the rationale and model for the importance of one's history and historical education and awareness. America celebrates itself in many rituals and traditions that are rooted in European tradition. The history books in the educational institutions from K–12 through college generously represent the European successes through various segments of history, while minimizing their travesties. As Bell Hooks states, "We should not begrudge them of celebrating themselves."[28]

The LINKS draw on that same premise of immersing the offender in African and African American history. The acts of betrayal reflected in the history along with the tradition of the collective are exposed. The LINKS strengthen the offender's resolve and intentions to strive toward the collective that places him in harmony with his spirituality, self-love, and self-control. This healthy, positive identity enables him to work in collaboration with his loved ones and society in positive and productive ways.

The next step in helping offenders answer the question, "How do I become what I want and need to be?" is positive reinforcement and nurturing information. The LINKS help offenders identify and eradicate the vestiges of the debilitating, corrosive, emasculating, and malignant information that produces feelings, beliefs, thoughts, and triggers of self-destruction, self-victimization, and displaced anger.

Many offenders tell us, "I want to do good but I keep ending up in these places (prisons). I want to change. I do not want to do the things that get me locked down, hurt my family, make me disappoint myself, and cause me to be a slave to addiction, violence, pain, disappointment, and incarceration." The LINKS help to erase the contaminated sources in the offender's mind and replace them with healthy, positive, and nurturing information, strategies, and techniques that are culturally specific and relevant to the African American male's life experiences.

In *The Psychology of Blacks: An African-Centered Perspective*, Parham, White, and Ajamu insist it is culturally imperative for African-American people to use themselves, their culture, and their history as the primary referent.[29] As the new, enriching, and comprehensive information is implanted, the men's self-esteem, self-respect, and self-confidence amass themselves into self-empowerment that establishes new personas and expanded repertoires of strategies for success. The offender becomes self-reliant, independent, positive in thought and behavior, and committed to a productive future in which he is the steward.

LINKS OF EMPOWERMENT MODULES

The offenders' answers to the question, "How do I maintain who I need to be for myself, my loved ones, and my community?" are developed through the LINKS four modules: **Safety**, **Belonging**, **Spirituality**, and **Positive Outcomes**. The modules are comprised of daily, weekly, monthly, and yearly practices of building inner strengths, which are utilized to develop a commitment to positive self-estem.

The Links of Empowerment are Safety, Belonging, Spirituality, and Positive Outcomes.

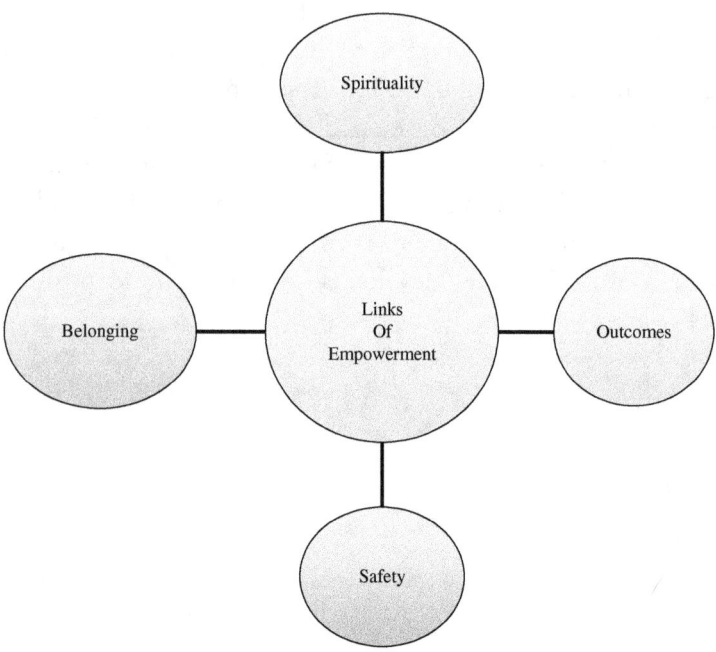

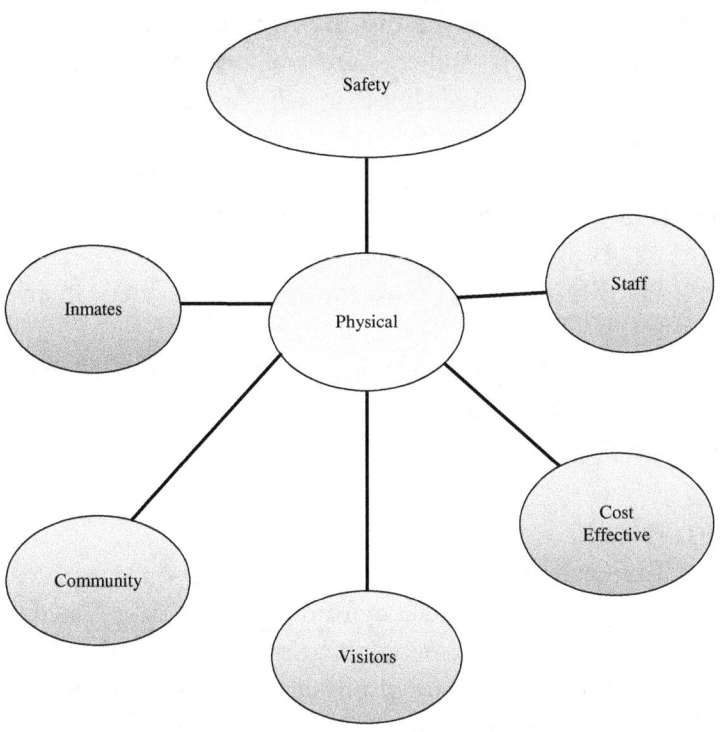

SAFETY

The mission statement of any correctional facility includes the goal of safety for the staff, inmates, and visitors. Safety must exist for the institution to operate effectively. The time, effort, and resources allocated to ensuring safety are enormous. Unfortunately, in the correctional environment, safety is based on a punitive model. This perpetuates a "them against us" philosophy. The punitive mode promotes divisiveness and encourages manipulation.

The LINKS of Empowerment improve safety in five categories: Physical, Staff, Inmates, Community, and Visitors. Higher levels of safety in institutions that have implemented the LINKS also provide increased levels in cost savings and cost effectiveness to these facilities.

Physical

To maximize his environment, a person must feel physically safe within that environment. The LINKS enable the offender to obtain mental maturity that transcends into physical safety. This state of physical safety encourages the offender to share his feelings of security with others. He is motivated to think and behave in ways that promote safety for himself and others.

When an inmate feels safe, he is more inclined to be cooperative, positive, productive, responsible, and futuristic. He does not have to devote an excessive amount of time and effort to physically protecting himself. A safe environment gives him the opportunity to concentrate his time and energy into rebuilding himself into a positive and productive individual. A safe environment enhances positive relationships among inmates and a willingness to collaborate on positive activities. Offenders interact with staff in healthy ways that build trust and collaborative efforts toward maintaining a safe environment for all.

Staff

The offender's feeling of safety ensures the safety of staff. Offenders will manage their thoughts and behavior in a way that reflects this sense of safety. The staff will recognize the positive way offenders are managing their time and effort. As a result, staff productivity and efficiency increases and the partnership between staff and offenders to achieve and maintain the goals of the organization is enhanced.

In a safe environment, staff stress will be reduced while their excitement and motivation to serve will increase and be maintained at a high level of performance. To staff, a safe environment means that they are valued by management and the offenders.

Inmates

The inmate's sense of safety is reflected in his mannerisms, communication, and actions. His growing commitment to a safe environment permeates everything in which he participates.

Offenders begin to spend more time and effort in positive programs and activities and less time in punitive activities such as conduct reports and confinement. Also, many more will work to compete for release and retention in the community.

Community

The surrounding community in which a facility is located is safer when offenders are in a safe environment. An offender that feels safe is not likely to escape or jeopardize his future.

Visitors

A safe environment for offenders translates into a safe environment for visitors. When visitors feel safe, they are more relaxed and experience more satisfaction while in the institution. Many make comments such as, "This does not feel like a prison." Visits with incarcerated family members and friends are more likely to be positive and complaints are minimized. Many inmates of the Circle Groups related that visits with love ones and friends are less stressful and more enjoyable. They believe it is due to the work in the Circle of facing their demons, owning responsibility, and having a plan for success.

COST EFFECTIVENESS

A safe offender means more money, time, and resources for staff and management to devote to areas that may not have received adequate attention. A safe environment is the best investment for an organization and offenders. The reduction in conduct reports means the correctional officer can devote his mind-set, energy, and time to assisting the offender in positive endeavors. Fewer conduct reports mean fewer hearings that require the time and effort of many other staff to conduct. As conduct reports are minimized, productivity and efficiencies increase, while stress decreases. Increased staff productivity leads to a decrease in the need for overtime, generating additional savings for the institution.

LINKS of Empowerment SAFETY EXERCISE for African American male offenders:

Describe what *safety* means to you.
What makes you feel safe?
What makes you feel unsafe?
When do you feel safe?
What do you do when you feel unsafe?
How do you make yourself feel safe?
How does your level of safety improve safety for others?
How does your level of feeling unsafe increase the level of danger for others around you?
What thoughts do you attach to safety?
How do those thoughts make you safe or unsafe?

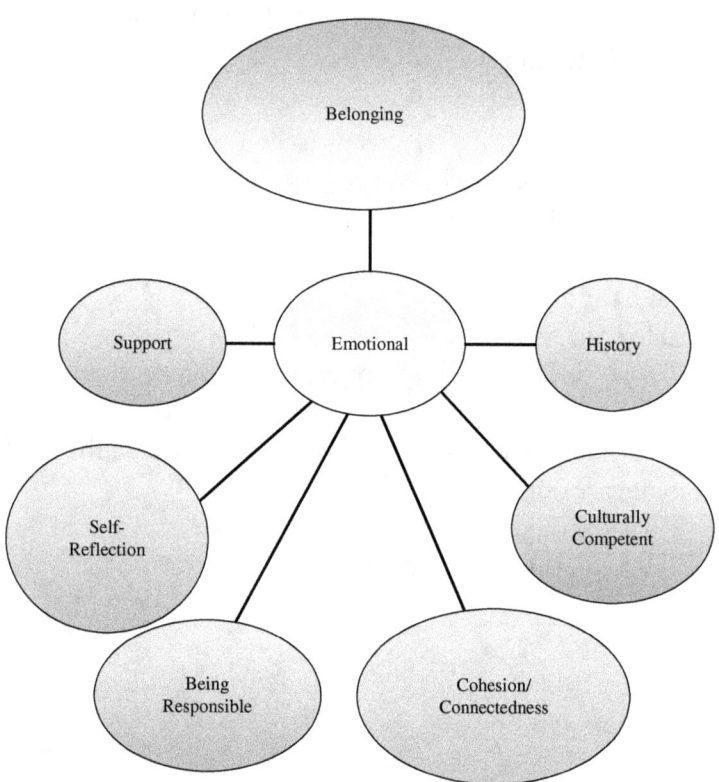

BELONGING

Human beings are social and have a need to feel connected to others. In the LINKS of Empowerment, the offender connects to his roots through African and African American history. The Circle of Empowerment Group, which is discussed in part 4 of this book, establishes a culturally specific normative standard for his existence and introspection. The group expectations are positive. These positive expectations guide the offender through his daily choices. The expectations set the bar at a level to create change in the offender's thinking and behaving.

As part of the Circle Group, the African American male offender connects to something larger and greater than himself. Baskin and Sommers believe this connection to something larger than the self (even in the name of self-help) appears to be a vital part of the desistance process (Baskin and Sommers, 1998, p. 137).

This gives him a sense of support and encouragement for his redefined way of life. He adjusts his habits to complement and strengthen the normative standards of the Circle Group. The repetitive practice of the group's norms becomes a lifestyle that offers him value and success. The offenders study and read in groups. The offenders model principles for each other.

In *What Blacks Owe to Each Other,* Randall Robinson states, "We are all mothered by culture and fathered by experience."[30] You connect to what you have become. The offender connects to information that portrays him as a positive contributor to society, with many successful role models who resemble him. He connects to a community that embraces his uniqueness, strengths, and hopes. As a member of the community, the offender is reminded of his responsibility to himself, his family, and his environment.

Belonging is as vital to African Americans as the air they breathe. Belonging is a fundamental concept in many traditional African rituals and traditions. Dr. Wade Nobles, a noted African psychologist, argues that belonging is so important that many of the African languages do not have words that convey individualism. Traditional western psychology accentuates the concepts of individualism, autonomy, and personal power as the highest form of human development.

Belonging is a community-based process in which all members are complete because they are a part of the whole. It expresses the concept, "I am because we are." This concept is similar to the widely spread African proverb, and title of Senator and former First Lady Hillary Clinton's book, It Takes a Village.[31]

African-centered programming teaches African American offenders about their collective identities, which is everlasting. This collective history develops a sense of self and belonging. In the African culture, belonging is the highest form of human development. Belonging develops a sense of mastery of the competencies needed to succeed in the major areas of life. Competition therefore is based on meeting the need of the collective group, as opposed to self-interest. A selfish perspective is viewed as a negative outcome, which brings shame on the collective. The collective process helps the men transfer this concept to their family members and community. They begin to connect how their actions can uplift their family as a unit and bond it toward a common purpose. The common purpose of thought, commitment and effort begins to be reflected in his children improving academically and their self-esteem improving in selecting friends with positive agendas.

Our African-centered approach is holistic. Guidance from the collective is considered a mandate. The greatest wisdom comes from the elders in the clan, group, or collective. It is the elder's responsibility to teach and guide, with persistence and accuracy, all those who come after them. The teaching includes finding a path back to the calm sense of self that is pure and consumed with self knowledge and love.

African writers speak of belonging to a collective, learning one's role in the collective, and respecting elders as vital to the growth process. Harmony is a prerequisite for the group relationship to evolve into a seamless process in which everyone has a place that is considered vital to the survival of the collective. Early African American history demonstrates this type of unity. The expression of unity among the slaves was difficult for slave holders. This unity was responsible for slave ships returning to Africa by captured Africans, slave revolts, and the like. To obliterate this unity, and consequently, the survival process, a slave master from the West Indies Willie Lynch published a document to teach and encourage other slaveholder's methodical control of the Africans. The infamous Willie Lynch[32] letter is a classic example of the measures slave owners took to disrupt the African's sense of belonging.

Knowing where one belongs develops safety and provides the support necessary for the healthy development of self. Thomas A. Parham believes that an individual's sense of belonging is a buffer against racism, bonds individuals of similar cultural practices, helps individuals adapt to environments more or less supportive of their cultural identity, breaks down barriers that hinder the development of genuine levels of intimacy, provides a sense of pride and achievement, and finally, enables individuals to relate to their past to visualize their future.[33]

Several factors impact—negatively or positively—the African American male offender's identity and sense of belonging. These factors are identified and integrated into the LINKS of Empowerment as follows.

Emotional Factor

The Emotional Factor is at the core of how a person sees himself in relation to his environment. There is a very strong connection between our beliefs about power and how we demonstrate power through our behavior. The behaviors can be adaptive or maladaptive. The strength-based empowerment theory recognizes that the emotional factor represents the feelings and life experiences that are attached to a person's soul. Feelings are created by our thoughts, which turn into stories of fear, fatalism, hopelessness, happiness, sadness, anxiety, and hope. The variety and intensity of these thoughts/feelings varies according to the individual's personal experiences. Many of these men could be thinking thoughts about their experiences that are not true. These untruths are ruling their lives, which places them on an emotional rollercoaster until they are able to create "emotional balance." Through self-knowledge and examining their thoughts, they can create understanding and acceptance of their responsibility for themselves and begin to achieve emotional development and maturity. History lessons provide models for evidence and reference. Author Byron Katie and her teachings in the "The Work" provide a simple process to review unexamined thoughts. The exercises help the men to find peace in the war zones of their minds. (Byron Katie)

Furthermore, specific readings and collective support enhances their ability to gain emotional balance. Their individual progress and that of their fellow Circle members provide the roadmap and reinforcement. They have developed a bond and trust that permeates throughout everything they do and say and provides the motivation for them to engage with the principles of the Circle.

Historical Factor

History denotes the origin of the person. It enables the person to understand themselves. It offers the African American male a legacy that contains the first civilization, inventors, and leaders. It connects him to a rich and glorious past. By knowing his history, the African American male offender can more effectively utilize the present. History provides a path to success. A belief of "I can" develops within the offender when he learns how his predecessors succeeded under greater burdens and obstacles. He learns the process to restore the calm.

The strength-based empowerment theory uses history as an essential tool in preparing the offender for a successful future. This knowledge provides insight, confidence, and motivation for the African American male to create a bright and productive future for himself and the world. He no longer lives inside his head with thoughts of self-destruction. He is able to find peace with all that is in the universe. He sees himself clearly, sometimes for the first time.

Cultural Factor

African American culture, values, and experience are the foundation for the LINKS of Empowerment. Strength-based empowerment theory materials and the Circle of Empowerment group processes are filtered through African American culture. Issues, topics, and solutions also are examined within this framework. The goal is to see oneself as many things which include being African American.

Support Factor

The Circle of Empowerment group process provides members with emotional support and encouragement. Members validate strengths and encourage healthy coping skills. Human beings isolate themselves and believe their stories are unique as opposed to similar to others'. When this happens, the stories, untruths, and half-truths take on a life of their own. When we see that others in the world are similar to us, we feel connected to them. This connection stops the internal war, which in turn stops the external war. There are no new stressful thoughts, only recycled ones.

Responsibility Factor

The primary group expectation is for members to be personally responsible for their thoughts and actions. The group does not accept a victim mindset. It helps each man examine the underlying motivation for his thoughts and actions. The Circle Group member is continuously guided toward the achievement of his positive goals by examining how each of his actions contributes to that achievement. As we learn who we are and see ourselves in others, we can finally start to treat others as we want to be treated. If we are treating ourselves with disdain, it is clear that we will project that disdain on others. Taking responsibility for ourselves includes all our thoughts. If we have loving and kind thoughts for ourselves, those will be projected in our behaviors. In turn, these behaviors become humane.

Self-Reflection Factor

Self-reflection enables the men to acknowledge and honor the similarities in their physical appearance, cultural background, and life experiences. The men are encouraged to accept these similarities as strengths in their self-development and to view them as critical to the oneness of the group. When we know ourselves there is no need to be defensive. When we hear criticism, we can turn inside and examine the thoughts to see if it is true or has ever been true and acknowledge it. We see our self-reflection in the projections that we place on others. The men come to learn that the thoughts they think about others are both about others and themselves. They see their mirror image in the faces of each other. This is very powerful and humbling. They are able to face themselves as they witness who they really are without the stories. A mirror is provided to them as a tool to look at themselves and report what it is that they see. They can finally take off the blinders and see themselves as never before. They face who they are without being what they have done. This process increases humanity.

Cohesion Factor

The group motto is: "I am because we are, and because we are, therefore, I am." This motto helps create a sense of family within the group. The impact of individual actions is acknowledged as having a direct impact on the solidarity and effectiveness of the group.

As we think so shall we be. This thought has been used frequently throughout many societies. African philosophy is to use the human experience to search for answers to unanswered questions. It is the reflection to look at oneself and others and make observations. Some of the tribes from the Sudan all have the same first and last name, including the men and women. When you are one there are no differences. If you think of yourself as part of something bigger, you begin to act as family with a greater sense of protection. This protection shows up in your interactions with all things in the world. We can wonder about the diversity and the unit in the universe. We can manage the wonder by taking on new habits and relationship with ourselves that demonstrate our knowledge that we are one family coexisting together in one world, on one planet fundamentally tied to each other in a very specific manner. The Circle of Empowerment uses scientific evidence to demonstrate to the coexisting relationships as evidence of the friendly cohesion of the world. The teachings of the Circle include the following:

> We are one world.
> We are one planet.
> We all breathe the same air.
> We can only eat what the earth produces.
> We can change our thoughts from believing untruths.
> We are our thoughts.
> Our behavior is created by our thoughts about ourselves and others.
> Our survival in the world is dependent upon each one of our behaviors toward each other.
> There are no victims, only events that happened to people.
> We are love.
> We are part of a friendly universe.
> We can use a simple process to change our thoughts and ultimately our behavior.
> I am because we are.

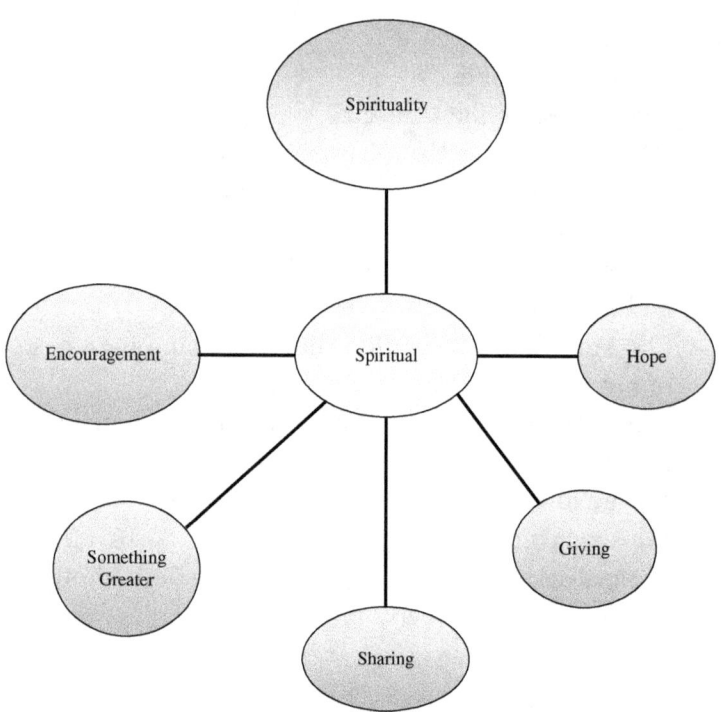

SPIRITUALITY

In Webster's dictionary, *spirit* is defined as, "a lively or brisk quality in a person or in a person's actions; a person having a character or disposition of a specified nature; or a mental disposition characterized by firmness or assertiveness, such as denied the charge with spirit." It is this sense of spirit that evolves into spirituality for the African American. It is widely believed that the spirituality of a black person is as much of them as is the blood that runs through his body. In *Counseling of Persons of African Decent: Raising the Bar of Practitioner Competence,* Thomas A. Parham said, "For many African cultures, science and spirituality are inextricably linked; spirituality is a reflection of science and science is a reflection of spirituality."[34] In the days of chattel slavery, the slaves' spirituality was their salvation for existing and coping. This mechanism, passed down through the centuries, has shielded African Americans from the hits of depletion, derailment, and destruction.

Spirituality has given African Americans something greater than themselves to believe in, to rely on, and to call on in times of trouble, pain, and fatalism. The belief in "something greater" provides support, encouragement, and peace. This inner peace gives comfort in the belief that "I" am worthy of existing and succeeding. It is the force that connects a person to his self-actualization and spiritual support system.

This spirituality recharges African American males so they can face another day of hits and challenges. It places the person's mind, body, and soul in harmony with the environment. From this African-centered perspective, spiritual survival is more important than physical survival.

Parham provides the following insight into the value and essence of spirituality in his book Counseling of Persons of African Descent:[35]

In the African cultural worldview, the essential ingredient and essence of everything, including humans, is spirit. To have spirit is to be imbued with life, a mind and soul, energy, force, passion, allegiances, and a guardian presence. It is the condition of being spirit, not merely practicing spirituality. The human being not only has spirit, he or she is spirit. In the African worldview, spirit has both real and symbolic meaning. It represents the divine spark which gives human beings their "(be)ingness; the essence of which becoming is an ongoing expression.

SPIRITUAL PRACTICES AND PRINCIPLES

The strength-based empowerment theory LINKS of Empowerment emphasizes four aspects of spirituality within the group process: Something Greater, Encouragement, Sharing, and Giving. Application involves the practice of the principles and beliefs that help a person be at peace with himself and in harmony with the external events of his environment. It is recognizing, cultivating, and reinforcing the positive power that dwells within, enhancing its manifestation in his thoughts, beliefs, and knowledge base.

Something Greater

Offenders build upon the belief that a power of goodness greater than themselves exists by learning to connect to this higher power through their thoughts and intentions, rituals, prayers, and actions. Each person holds beliefs about God. The Circle of Empowerment help the offenders expand their concept to include the separation between what God has responsibility for and their own responsibility. It separates the duties and the focus. Through the exercises, the participants start to see where their thoughts have taken them into areas that cause them suffering as it relates to God. They can build trust that the universe is friendly and in order. They can join mankind with self-knowledge and trust in themselves and the worldly events that have caused them great grief in the past. However, the victimization in the African American community are plentiful. These stories stored in the mind of the community cause terror, fear, and internal destruction. They are projected into the future as truths and are used to justify more unkind thoughts and behaviors. This vicious and insidious cycle traps people into a life without joy.

Trusting something greater than you therefore becomes essential to the work in the Circle of Empowerment. Trusting that your needs will get met and that you are essential to society becomes of great importance.

Encouragement

The Circle Group's primary focus is to provide encouragement by reframing everything in a way that taps into the member's strengths and goals.

Sharing

The group promotes sharing life experiences, strengths, encouragement, love, hope, demons, motivation, successes, challenges, pain, happiness, frustrations, and a sense of oneness.

Giving

Each member is expected to use his positive energy for the betterment of every member. Giving is essential to the progress of the collective. The motto is: "Giving builds strong and positive character, and the more you give to others, the more your blessings multiply." The individual member's level of giving represents his level of maturity, confidence, and responsibility.

Hope

The support, validation, and encouragement supplied by the group's connectedness and oneness rekindle hope in each man. The offender reduces his fear, building his optimism and courage to a level that empowers him to have hope and commit to this hope through his daily actions.

POSITIVE OUTCOMES

This fourth module refocuses the offender's positive energy through: re-socialization, self-awareness, self-control, positive role modeling, and responsible behavior to generate positive outcomes. The offender's mental and social growth is validated. It provides correctional facilities with concrete benchmarks to measure the inmate's progress in becoming a productive and cooperative individual.

The offender who responds favorably to this program will begin to show a more positive attitude about life and himself. He will be self-motivated and self-controlled. He will associate with other positive persons. He will avoid conduct reports. He will be a conciliator in potentially volatile situations. He will lead by example in positive ways. He will mentor other offenders on living a positive and productive lifestyle. He will develop positive habits such as reading, and physical fitness; and participate in job training, therapeutic treatment, and release planning opportunities. He will be an asset to himself, the authorities, his family, and society.

Re-Socialization

Through the strength-based empowerment theory LINKS, the offender is re-socialized into a positive, responsible, accountable, and productive individual who is committed to healthy relationships with society, his family, and his community. The results of our program diminish the offender's negativity through healthy, positive, and cultural specific information to guide the offender in his reclamation.

Self-Awareness

The offender's new positive self-awareness will guide him to employ his energies in industrious ways. His acknowledgement of valuing himself will be replicated in his thinking and behavior. The enlightening cultural specific information will encourage the offender to devote more of his time and effort in ways to honor his heritage.

The offender is immersed in the culturally specific history on which he establishes his origin as a human being. The historical information widens his understanding of his cultural connection. He internalizes this information and processes it into hope, motivation, courage, and commitment to a better way of life.

Self-Control

The program is organized to help the offender recognize and achieve the level of self-control that enables him to be positive, productive, and in harmony with his environment. The offender's self-control increases in relation to the amount of knowledge he obtains. The offender develops an internal desire to be self-controlled because it represents how he respects and values himself.

Positive Role Modeling

The LINKS of Empowerment presents the offender with many African American achievers as role models. It shows the offender how to live a positive and productive lifestyle while managing the challenges and disappointments of life. The offender can employ some of the same strategies and techniques provided by these heroes and heroines.

Responsible Behavior

Responsible behavior is the culmination of the program's influence on the offender. His thoughts and behavior reflect a sense of responsibility. Responsible behavior produces positive results that encourage the offender to commit to this new lifestyle fully. This generates more success and support for the offender.

AUTHENTIC POWER

In his book, *Soul Stories,* Gary Zukav discusses "authentic power." It is power of feeling good and feeling fulfilled. It gives one meaning and purpose. The person is happy to be alive and has a reason to be alive. Everything one does is joyful and exciting. A person looks forward to each day and each night.[36]

The LINKS of Empowerment enables African American male offenders to achieve the authentic power of which Gary speaks. Self-empowerment is achieved through internal development, growth, and maturity. The LINKS enable the person to harness their true power that comes from within the soul, through the education of the mind, the healthy development and application of emotions, self-control, and effective decision-making. The correctional environment is like an enormous magnifier for victimizing African American male offenders. It is a vivid and constant reminder of the dehumanizing and degrading realities of what it is to be African American and male in America. It takes powerful information, trust, bonding, support, reprogramming, and redirection to balance their fears, apprehensions, vulnerability, and feelings of oppression.

The LINKS of Empowerment are based on the power of the individual to harness the power of faith, hope, self-determination, self-empowerment, self-control, and self-awareness. The LINKS provide the offender with stability in thought, feelings, and behavior. It enables the offender to anticipate and assess situations that activate his negative reactive behavior. It helps the offender avoid victimization and make choices that empower him psychologically and socially.

The LINKS are anchored by the authentic power of the temple, called the body. Participants are taught that the body is their temple, and that within this temple is the true source of power and peace. They are encouraged to develop and call upon the authentic power that lives inside of them. Offenders come to understand and accept that inner peace and value are the seeds to genuine power and that external validation is not the source of genuine power.

The LINKS remind the offender that what exist in the soul and mind gets expressed externally. If love dwells in a man's soul, then this is what will flow out of him. The offender makes a commitment to self-love because he learns this is the first requirement to showing genuine love to others. He is counseled that self-love must genuinely exist within him so that he can be a positive member of the larger group.

The offender goes through an exercise where they draw a circle on a sheet of paper. The circle represents them. Then they place in proximity to the circle the people they love. Invariably, they place family members closer to the circle (them) than their friends. They are then asked who did they spend most of their time with when they were in the community and who were they with when they did their crime(s). Again it is predictable that they were with their friends most of time when they were in the community and when they did their crime(s). When they are shown that by their own illustration that the people they placed closest to the circle were not the individuals toward whom they devoted the majority of time and effort, they begin to rationalize their behavior. However, this exercise clearly reveals to them and their fellow Circle members that their management of time and effort needs to drastically change if they value the relationships they drew.

They are asked to develop ways that they can achieve the illustration they developed. After this they get into small groups and discuss their plans of action. Someone records the consensus at which the group arrives. They come back into larger groups, and each group reports. Once a month, the men get into their small groups and then the main group to repeat the exercise. This is a very important activity because it provides a crucial transferable skill that men will use through their life. They have to constantly review their actions and thoughts in relationship to people they claim they love the most. It is not about their loved ones but about the men assuming their responsibility to have their actions replicate their commitment.

Family is extremely important in the African American culture, and this exercise honors that and re-emphasizes that the whole is greater and more significant than individual. The men are able to discuss manhood, fatherhood, husbandry, loyalty, friendships, relationships, obligation, etc.

PART 4

THE CIRCLE
OF EMPOWERMENT

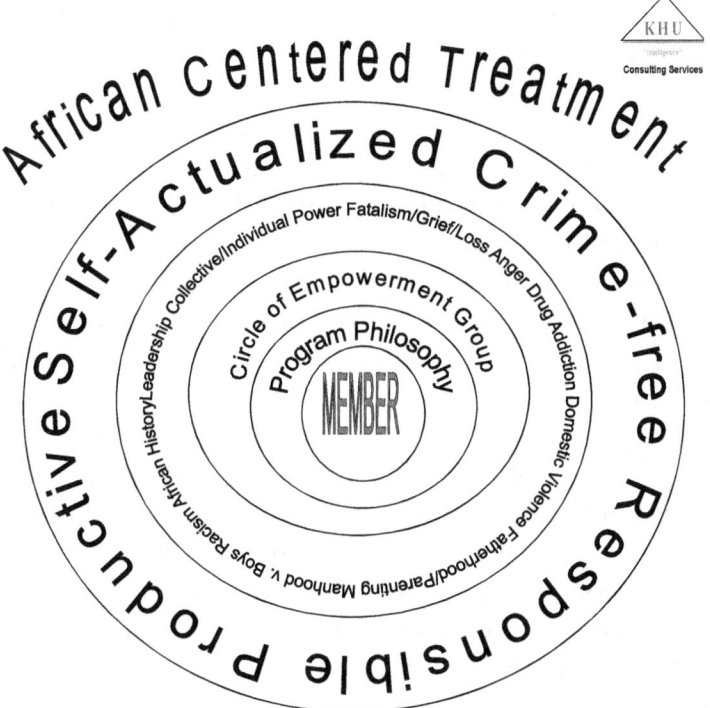

African centered Treatment

KHU
"intelligence"
Consulting Services

Self-Actualized Crime-free

Responsible Productive

Circle of Empowerment Group

Program Philosophy

MEMBER

Collective/Individual Power Fatalism/Grief/Loss Anger Drug Addiction Domestic Violence Manhood v. Boys Racism African History Leadership Fatherhood/Parenting

The Circle of Empowerment is a support group that harnesses the knowledge, energy, talents, and commitment of offenders to focus on positive self-development, personal accountability, and positive lifestyle. It empowers the offender to effectively manage his life choices and to maximize opportunities for progress. Through support and unity of purpose and effort, offenders achieve personal growth and insight, acquire tools for living a crime-free lifestyle, and develop positive habits.

The cultural responsiveness of the Circle of Empowerment provides the African American offender a strong foundation for connecting to his roots of origin, his history of evolving, and better understanding of his present environment. It builds individual pride that adds to collective pride and respect. The culturally sensitive group provides for the sharing of common styles of thinking and knowing.

The Circle of Empowerment focuses on the uniqueness of the African American male offender and helps the offender to de-program his mind from thoughts and information of negativism, self-destruction, fatalism, and homicidal tendencies, and to replenish his mind with cultural responsive knowledge. It encourages the offender to look at his life as being a gift of hope. Offenders are guided from looking for excuses to justify their station in life to accepting personal responsibility that will provide strength-based development and empowerment. The principles of the Circle of Empowerment are designed to provide guidance for the offender's thought and decision-making processes, which leads to success. The principles enhance personal responsibility and accountability. They provide the offender a method for assessing his progress and a framework for achievement. These tools help the offender better navigate through the challenges in life, helping him to achieve balance between his spirit, mind, and body and to connect the past with the present to formulate a fulfilling future.

The Circle of Empowerment process is discussed within the group on a regular basis to ensure that its premises and goals are being met. The members regularly perform self-assessments to gauge their progress. As the group matures, it becomes responsible for itself and the self-assessment of the members.

Through the African oral tradition, offenders communicate their life story. One of the best ways to understand a particular subculture or group at a particular point in time is to analyze the stories that members of that group are telling.

The Circle of Empowerment Group constantly reminds participants that it offers a positive lifestyle that is crime-free, positive, and successful. Success is the aim of the Circle philosophy. Participants learn that the mind is the key to their success and that their most powerful tool is the ability to make good choices.

Mind is the Source

Mind is the Source

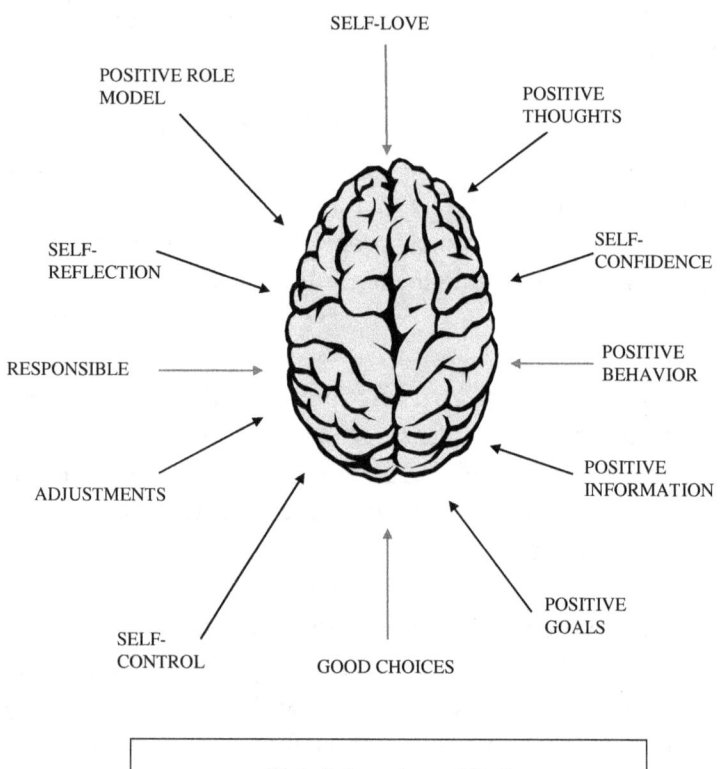

SELF-LOVE

POSITIVE ROLE MODEL

POSITIVE THOUGHTS

SELF-REFLECTION

SELF-CONFIDENCE

RESPONSIBLE

POSITIVE BEHAVIOR

ADJUSTMENTS

POSITIVE INFORMATION

POSITIVE GOALS

SELF-CONTROL

GOOD CHOICES

Choice is the most powerful tool

GROUP STRUCTURE

The group structure lends itself to the communal and collective culture of African Americans. It connects the offender to family, peer group, and community. It provides for unity of purpose and effort. It offers the offender something greater than himself.

The meeting structure enables the offender to learn, practice, and embody the principles of order, respect, trust, support, feedback, introspection, and reflection. The routine is repetitive and hands-on. It responds to the spirituality of African Americans through various rituals.

The Circle of Empowerment Group encourages human touch among the offenders in a positive and nurturing way. Most African American males are socialized in ways that promote detachment, destruction, and disillusionment. These male offenders rarely touch in positive ways in a corrections or confinement environment. Touching in healthy, acceptable, and supportive ways helps the offenders redefine male bonding.

In this section, we will examine how to facilitate a Circle Group in your facility. Remember that the strength-based empowerment theory is an African-centered program geared specifically toward the African American male. The actual structure and procedures of the group, however, may be altered to meet the needs of any specific group.

I. GROUP PROCEDURES AND RITUALS

Opening chant: recited in a circle holding hands with the right over the left.

Creed: recited in unison.

Giving thanks: each person gives thanks to those who have made positive contributions in his life in the past and in the present.

Libations: individuals kneel while pouring water into a plant.

Circle Poem: recited while seated in a circle.

Introduction of visitors.

Check: Each person shares a story of success or relates a problem to receive guidance.

Spiritual Reading or Message.

Meeting Topic: article, book report, holiday celebration.

Closing Chant

Opening Chant

I will achieve! You will achieve! We will achieve!

The chairs are arranged in a circle to get the meeting underway. All members participate in the arrangement of the chairs for the meeting. The men stand in a circle, hands clasped in front of them, with the right arm over the left to recite the opening chant. As each man makes eye contact with the man standing directly across from him in the circle, the chant begins with all arms rising and falling in unison.

At the conclusion of the chant, the men perform "shaking it up" by moving their clasped hands in a circular motion. The significance of this is shaking up the spirit, the unity, the support, the hope, and the motivation for being involved in the group itself. This is the begins the process of purifying the mind, recharging life batteries, recommitting efforts to living a responsible lifestyle, and owning the power to make a positive impact on the world. Because African culture emphasizes oral tradition, the chant, like the entire Circle Group process, relies heavily on verbal participation.

Creed

For the reciting of the creed, Circle Group members arrange themselves in a circle with their arms interlocked, and they recite the creed in unison.

Creed of the Circle

Our people may stand
On the broad and powerful shoulders
Of the African American males
Who take pride in their people
We prepare our children for success
We will sacrifice for our people 's freedom
We will break down the barriers of injustice
We will open the doors of opportunity
That our people may walk through.
We will provide our shoulders for support
Our arms for protection
Our minds to capture a successful future
And our role modeling for guidance

Giving Thanks

Circle Group members then unlock arms and again hold hands. This can be very challenging for black males initially, but the experience is rewarding. The human touch is important to recovery, accepting support, being open to change, and making progress. Each Circle Group member then gives thanks to those who have made a positive impact in his life in the past or presently and then gives thanks to a higher power.

In groups of forty or more men, the "popcorn thanks" method is applied. Each individual calls out one word of gratitude, such as hope, inspiration, commitment, accountability, thanks, or love. This type of call and response activity fills the room with encouragement, validating each individual's feelings of unity and giving the group a sense of oneness.

Libations

Libation, as defined in the Webster, is the act of pouring a liquid as a sacrifice to a deity. Therefore, it is the spiritual leader of the group who performs this act as an African tradition of giving thanks, honoring your ancestors, and recognizing your spirituality. The spiritual leader kneels while pouring water into a plant while group members stand around to observe and the libation portion of the Circle Group is completed.

Check-In

Circle Group members then return to their seats and the president of the Circle Group reads the Circle poem. Each member shares an accomplishment achieved since the last meeting. Achievements may include being free of conduct problems, contacting a family member, or even passing one the tests toward receiving a General Education Diploma. Not only does this activity encourage positive behavior through recognition, it also gets Circle Group members into the habit of working on their personal goals and developing achievements.

Spiritual Reading or Message

The spiritual leader is someone who the rest of the Circle Group members respect and value due to his level of spirituality and maturity. The spiritual leader reads a scripture or provides the group with an uplifting message relevant to some of their personal struggles and provides them support to make sound decisions.

Meeting Topic

The Circle Group leaders predetermine the topic of the meeting. The topic can be from a newspaper, book, book report, or an actual presentation from a guest. The topic discussed should be relevant to the issues faced by the men in the Circle Group and can be politically, socially, or spiritually driven.

Closing Chant

The meeting is concluded with the men standing in a circle with their hands interlocked. Again, the significance of African-centered unity is emphasized with the use of the circle. The group leader gives the men some words of encouragement, and the group then recites the closing chant three times: "I will be strong for my brothers and sisters" and this concludes the meeting.

II. PARTICIPATION EXPECTATIONS

Participation in the Circle Group should be open to all inmates in any given correctional facility. The emphasis, however, remains focused on the plight of the African American male offender. The approach and strategy promoted by the Circle Group are applicable to any offender. This is why all groups are encouraged to maintain diversity at all times. Participation is voluntary. However, once an individual makes a commitment to join and participate in the Circle Group, he is expected to attend all meetings and arrive to all meetings on time. Late arrivers must express sorrow for being late with the understanding that promptness is the beginning of a healthy lifestyle. The use of foul or derogatory language based on ethnicity, gender, or lifestyle is unacceptable. Inmates have to learn how to provide positive feedback from a prospective that strives toward self-accountability.

The Circle Group promotes the minimization of excuses and examines obstacles and challenges as footsteps to success and developing proper character. Circle Group participation directs the inmate's attention on self-development, self-determination, and self-accountability. The inmate is encouraged to see obstacles, determine alternative solutions that keep him in a winning position, and commit to a course of action to keep him in control of his destiny. The inmate is encouraged to widen his commitment to include those he claims to love, and let his decisions and his actions be the measurement of love.

Library

Each Circle Group must have its own library separate from that of the facility. Circle Groups members are required to read extensively on the history of Africans, African Americans and African influence on other cultures. Circle Group members must be provided with readings on self-development, fatherhood, relationships, parenting, anger management, chemical abuse and recovery, physical abuse, and decision-making tactics.

Circle Group members will participate in reading and study circles to promote reading and provide the opportunity to discuss topics, thus helping Circle Group members gain a better understanding of any given topic and its applications. Each library must contain at least two copies of the following:

- The Destruction of Black Civilization by Chancellor Williams
- The Psychology of Blacks: An African-Centered Perspective by Thomas A. Parham, L. White, and Adisa Ajamu
- Psychological Storms, The African American Struggle for Identity by Thomas A. Parham
- Breaking the Psychological Slavery, and Natural Psychology and Human transformation by Na'im Akbar
- Black Men: Obsolete, Single, Dangerous, by Haki R. Madhubuti
- State of Emergency: We Must Save African American Males

- Black Economics: Solutions for Economic and Community Empowerment
- Hip Hop vs. MART: A Psycho/Social Analysis of Values, by Jawanza Kunjufu
- Critical Issues in Educating African American Youth for Success, by Jawanza Kunjufu
- Countering the Conspiracy to Destroy Black Boys, by Jawanza Iunjufu
- The Psychodynamics of Black Self-Annihilation in Service of white Domination by Amos N. Wilson
- The Falsification of African Consciousness by Amos N. Anderson
- Black Skin White Mask by Franz Fanon
- Faith of Our Fathers: African American Men Reflect on Fatherhood edited by Abdre C. Willis
- African Power: Affirming African Indigenous Socialization in the Face of the Culture Wars by Asa G. Hillard, III, and Nana Baffout Amankwatia
- The Emperor's New Clothes: Biological Theories of Race at the Millenium by Joseph L., Jr. Graves (Paperback - Feb 2003)
- African Psychology by Wade N. Nobles
- Each Night I Die by David Belton
- Faces at the Bottom of the Well by Derrick Bell
- Black Pearls by Eric V. Copage;
- Killing Rage: Ending Racism by Bell Hooks
- The Spirit of a Man by Iyanla Vanzant
- Two Nations: Black and White, Separate, Hostile, Unequal by Andrew Hacker
- The Rage of a Privileged Race and Color-Blind: Seeing Beyond Race in a Race Obsessed World by Ellis Cose

- The Mis-Education of the Negro by Carter G. Woodson
- The Guide to Male Parenting by Earl Ofair Hutchinson
- Between God **and** Gangsta Rap: Bearing Witness to Black Culture by Michael Eric Dyson
- Healing Racism in America: A Prescription for the Disease by Nathan Rutstein
- A New Earth-Awakening to Your Life's Purpose by Eckhart Tolle
- I need Your Love-Is That True? By Byron Katie

Choir

Many Circle Groups establish a choir that performs before the general inmate population and at events such as staff retirements, holiday celebrations, Victim Awareness Month, and Women's Appreciation Month. Participation in the choir taps into the natural talents of many Circle Group members and reinforces the idea of the whole being more important than the individual. Circle Group choirs are currently striving toward being awarded the privilege to perform in communities.

Kwanzaa and Black History Month

Circle Group members are required to celebrate Kwanzaa. During the celebration, each Circle Group member is obligated to perform some discipline of Kwanzaa at each of the Circle Group meetings held in that month. During the month of February, each Circle Group member is required to do an extensive book report on any influential African or African American using at least two sources of literature, pick a song from an African or African

American musician to play on stereo, and read a piece of literature from African or African American to read aloud to the group.

Newsletter

The Circle Group also has a monthly newsletter for distribution to all Circle Groups. The inmates write most of the articles. Individual Circle Groups create and publish newsletters that focus on the activities of the particular group. The newsletter is a vehicle for sharing information amongst the many Circle Groups, maintaining commonality, and promoting innovation.

III. ACTIVITIES

In this final section, we will discuss some of the social issues African American males face in their communities as well as in institutional settings. We will also examine how to use these topics for discussion in the Circle Group along with activities for the Circle Group members to do relevant to these topics.

The first topic we will examine is *racism.* The Webster defines "racism" as" the belief that race is the primary determinant of human traits and capacities and that racial differences produce an inherent superiority of a particular race." Racism permeates in the world and is life altering. It can cause severe psychological damage. Learning to deal with racism is a skill. In communities and in public school systems, black males are being labeled behaviorally challenged, disordered, attention deficit disordered and oppositionally defiant.

These labels cause the individual to be treated differently or "special." For example, students who have these labels placed upon them are expected to do much less work or work of lower quality than other students, placing them at social disadvantage. Many of these same children are exposed, in their homes and communities, to high levels of unemployment, violence, alcoholism, and all the other diseases that plague poor black communities.

African American male inmate struggle to maintain themselves behind prison walls. They have to deal with racism on a daily basis in an environment that is hostile and anti-human, and anger is often their initial response. Anger is a mask for the true feelings of fear, hurt, and powerlessness experienced by a victim of racism and is frequently misunderstood. Racism and how to cope with racism are topics that must be examined thoroughly in the Circle Group.

IV. GROUP DISCUSSION TOPICS

Discussion Topic: Racism

Exercise:

Discuss instances where you felt your race was the major determinant in how you were treated. How did this make you feel, and what was your reaction toward the individual who was being racist? Now that you have grown as an individual, discuss what you should have done differently. If you did nothing, discuss what you feel would have been the best solution to defuse the issue.

Questions: What is "racism"?

How do you deal with it when you feel someone is being racist toward you? Why is anger not a plausible response to the disease of racism?

Has there been an incident in which you prejudged someone based on how they looked? If so, what about the individual made you feel this way? When you hear the word "racism," do you only think "black and white"? How is racism perpetuated in your community?

Discussion topic: Manhood vs. Boyhood

"Manhood" is described as "the condition of being an adult male as distinguished from a child or female." A major problem in the African American community is lack of positive male role models. It is difficult to determine what manhood really is when you have never been given any admirable examples. In his book, *Each Night I Die,* David Belton emphasizes the differences in manhood versus boyhood:

Men are responsible; boys are irresponsible. Men elevate their women; boys debase them in the name of deception and false love. Men see an obstacle as a challenge; boys see it as a stumbling block. Men take advantage of today; boys delay things until a later date, however, seldom is anything accomplished. Men have visions of the future; boys have stale dreams of the past. Men have priorities; boys take life as it comes.

Readings:
Breaking the Chains Psychological Slavery by Na'im Akbar, *Each Night I Die by* David Belton

Exercise:
Write your definition of manhood. Describe how your definition of manhood compared with your behavior while in the community. Then make two columns-Positives and Negatives. Based on how you behaved in the community, indicate under each column the positive and negatives. Then count the positives and negatives. Explain then why you think you have more than the other or they are equal. If you have more negatives than positives, indicate what you think you need to do to get more positives.

The next topic we will examine is the ***emasculation*** of African American males. Webster defines *emasculate* as "to deprive of strength, vigor, or spirit" and "to deprive of virility or procreative power." Emasculation is directly related to the topic of racism and should be discussed cooperatively. Each Circle Group member will write the definition of "emasculate." Then the Circle Group members must write down and recite the following poem in order to grasp a better understanding of racism and emasculation and how the two correlate.

Emasculating
Emasculating is your description of me.
Emasculating is your portrayal of me.
Emasculating is your treatment of me.
Emasculating is your renunciation of my humanity.
Emasculating is your repugnance of me.
Emasculating is your repudiation of my contributions.
Emasculating is your abomination against me.
Emasculating is your malignant neglect of me.
Genocidal are your atrocities against me.
Genocidal are your acts of carnage against me.
Genocidal are your trickeries against my existence.
Genocidal are your entitlements that hinder my liberties, my freedoms, my potential.
Emasculating me to ensure your safety.
Emasculating me to ensure your dominance.
Emasculating me to ensure your comfort.
Emasculating me to ensure your existence.
Emasculating me but I still survive.
Emasculating my spirit but still I cope.
Emasculating my efforts but still I strive.
Emasculating my economic stability but still I provide.

Jerry Smith

An overwhelming percentage of African American males have a misguided, negative, and destructive perception and history of performance that is an immature, unhealthy, and unsuccessful model of manhood. This has created a mutated framework of manhood that is based on fear, external control, hopelessness, failure, emasculation, internalized racism, and immediate material gratification.

The model of manhood for many young African American males is extracted from their peers and the media. Since the 1970s, the African American male has been depicted as a criminal of some sort in movies and on television. For example, in the Oscar award winning film, *Training Day*, the main character, played by Denzel Washington, is a crooked police officer who is taken down by not only a white inferior officer but the Russian Mafia as well. America's number one enemy during the Cold War was depicted in this film as a hero against the incorrigible, criminal minded, socio-pathetic African American male.

The gangsta rap has overtaken the African American and American culture. Rap recording artists are paid generously to promote thuggish and irresponsible behavior along with demeaning African American females in lyrics. Rappers also encourage the emasculation of the African American male in the way they dress in white T-shirts that come down past the knee.

Another example in movies of the emasculation of the African American male is the film, *To Wong Fu*, where

Wesley Snipes plays a drag queen and is never seen throughout the movie as a real man. Because of these distortions in the depiction of the African American male, many young black men do not possess the capacity to recognize or authenticate positive role models in their sphere of living. The African American male has been programmed to look for artificial sources for their knowledge, guidance, and validation.

True and natural knowledge unravels this confusion, providing order, understanding, balance, and harmony to the spirit. When you are under the control of someone else's scheme of self-gratification and survival, true and natural knowledge is obscured from penetrating your life. You psychologically and physically reject any intrusion or infusion of true and natural knowledge, leaving yourself vulnerable to grafted knowledge.

Your words and behavior are the first signs of mental illness. You may find yourself accepting and promoting violent behavior, disrespecting your family, and separating yourself from them to build bonds with less-desirable individuals, developing poor habits, practicing self-medication, procreating irresponsibly, and seeking power the wrong way just to provide you with a sense of manhood.

In order to abolish this revolving door of emasculation, you must redefine yourself and your manhood in positive ways. Once you do this using an African-centered perspective, a foundation of manhood that is in alignment with your true and natural knowledge is built.

African-centered knowledge compliments your social and cultural experiences, helping to redefine your manhood and better equip you with sound decision-making skills, which allow you to better assess your adherence to your redefined manhood. This redefinition of self enables you to develop nurturing and enriching principles for living that provide protection against destruction, discouragement, and derailment. As your sense of manhood increases, you mature as an individual and you are able to be an admirable steward of yourself while being a positive role model for others.

After discussing the issue, Circle Group members must copy and recite the following poem:

Manhood is self-education to achieve a healthy and comprehensive self-awareness.

Manhood is being responsible in thought and behavior.

Manhood is making your responsibilities a priority over personal desires.

Manhood is assuming personal responsibility for decisions made and behavior.

Manhood is rejecting enticements that lead to self-destruction.

Manhood is self-love and self-appreciation with humility.

Manhood is understanding and being in alignment with the natural order of things.

Manhood is being self-controlled.

Manhood is patience in spite of disappointments.

Manhood is managing the challenges of life without collapsing.

Manhood is understanding that challenges build character.

Manhood is not using inequality or disappointment as an excuse for irresponsibility.

Manhood is being self-sufficient. Manhood is believing in something greater than yourself.

Discussion Topic: Manhood vs. Boyhood

Reading: Breaking the Chains of Psychological Slavery by Na'im Akbar

Exercise:

Write your definition of manhood. Describe how your definition of manhood compares with your behavior while in the community. Make a positive and negative column, and count the number in each. Explain why you have more in one column than the other or equal amounts. If you have more negatives, indicate what you need to do to add to the list of positives.

Questions:

How do you define manhood?

What do you think influenced your definition of manhood? What are the strengths in how you practice your manhood?

What fears do you have about meeting your responsibilities as a man? How does society help you achieve your definition of manhood?

How does society make it difficult to achieve your definition of manhood?

Flowing right out of the topic of manhood versus boyhood is the topic of *fatherhood.* Webster defines *a father* as "one that originates or institutes" or "a man who has begotten a child." Fatherhood is essential to the spirit and complete development of African American males. The absence of a father has caused many African American males to be lost, chained to fear, violent, and directionless.

A father is a leading citizen who establishes and maintains a constructive and supportive relationship with all children, biological or not, for whom he assumes responsibility. Fatherhood is a life-long process of providing care, guidance, and protection for these children. The greatest problem facing the black community in America is the absence of father figures in the home, community, or church.

Discussion Topic: Fatherhood

Readings:
Black Fatherhood by Earl Hutchinson
What it Means to Be a Daddy: Fatherhood for Black Men Away from Their Children by Jennifer Her
Faith of our Fathers: African American on Fatherhood edited by Andre C. Willis
State of Emergency: We Must Save Our African American Males by Jawanza Kunjufu
Counseling Persons of African Descent by Michael Connor

Questions:
How do you define fatherhood?
What are your expectations as a father?

What are the barriers preventing you from meeting your parenting expectations? How can you be a positive role model for your children if you are in prison?

What was your relationship like with your father?

How does your relationship with your father influence the way you parent? What can you do to be a better father?

What kind of relationship do you want to have with your children?

What are the barriers to parenting your children when the mother is involved in another relationship?

A very sensitive topic of discussion is domestic violence. It is defined in two parts: "domestic" meaning "of or relating to the household or family" and "violence" meaning "intense, turbulent, or furious, often destructive action or force. Most African American males have witnessed, been the victim of, or even participated in the act of domestic violence.

Discussion Topic: Domestic Violence

Reading: Black Family Violence by Robert L. Hampton

Exercise: Discuss

Domestic violence is considered physical and/or emotional abuse. Domestic violence occurs when one person controls another person by fear or physical and psychological strain. At one time, domestic violence was legal in the United States. Men were allowed to discipline their families by the use of a stick no wider than their thumb.

Questions:

What did men gain from this kind of control?

What did they lose?

Why did the law change?

What does partnership mean to you?

Are you in a real relationship if you control the other person?

What happens to children who witness domestic violence? Who were your models for violence as a child?

What lesson did you learn?

How do you stop yourself from being violent?

Can you be addicted to violence? Explain.

Does violent behavior prove your manhood?

What is the connection between unemployment, alcoholism, and black family violence?

Chemical addiction is another serious problem in the African American community. It is defined as the "compulsive need for and use of a habit-forming substance characterized by tolerance and well-defined physiological symptoms upon withdrawal." The causes of chemical addiction in the African American male are the feelings of hopelessness and helplessness and inadequacies in manhood and fatherhood. An addict will kill, steal, and even prostitute himself to achieve that small gratification of getting high.

Discussion Topic: Chemical Addiction

Exercise: Discuss

Addiction is the first problem we need to address before we can make meaningful lasting progress in solving other problems. Many African Americans come into treatment later than their white counterparts, and most go through treatment because of court orders. Addiction is one of the strongest forms of slavery. Drug use is a form of fatalism, and drug dealing is a way to feel powerful. Drug use and distribution are seen as ways to lash out at the system. But selling and using drugs have a negative effect on the community.

Questions:

What is the relationship between self-hate and drug addiction?

What other feelings are gratified by the use of drugs?

Why are drugs so accessible in black communities?

The final topic for discussion is emotion, which is defined simply as "mental state." African American males, in particular, have difficulty expressing their emotions. They may feel such discussions are feminine or weak. But they need to be able to decipher what emotions caused them to be incarcerated and how to control those emotions. They also need to know that having emotions is not necessarily feminine, but that it is human to feel.

Discussion Topic: Emotions

Definitions: Read aloud

Feelings: activities,   awareness,   consciousness, enjoyment, excitability, to feel, motor response, pain, perception, to believe, inclination, point of view, emotion, mood, aura, reflex, reaction

Drive: ambition, action, surge, move

Pain: afflict, anguish, harm, injure, irritate, discomfort

Numb: aloof, dazed, stupefied

Longing: ambition, craving, ravenous, thirst, ardent

Insecure: afraid, apprehensive, unreliable, loose, immature

Secure: able, confident, well-founded, undamaged

Fear: abhorrence, panic, terror, fright, distress

Free Will: intent, consent, choice, freedom

Need: commitment, lack, duty, essential, requisite

Distortion: alter, mangle, misinterpretation

Belong: appertain, attach, akin, permeate

Anger: madness, outrage, scared, fury

Defensive: averting, arresting, opposing

Fatalism: a doctrine that events are fixed in advance so that human beings are powerless to change

Grief: an unfortunate outcome

Loss: failure to gain, win, obtain, or utilize

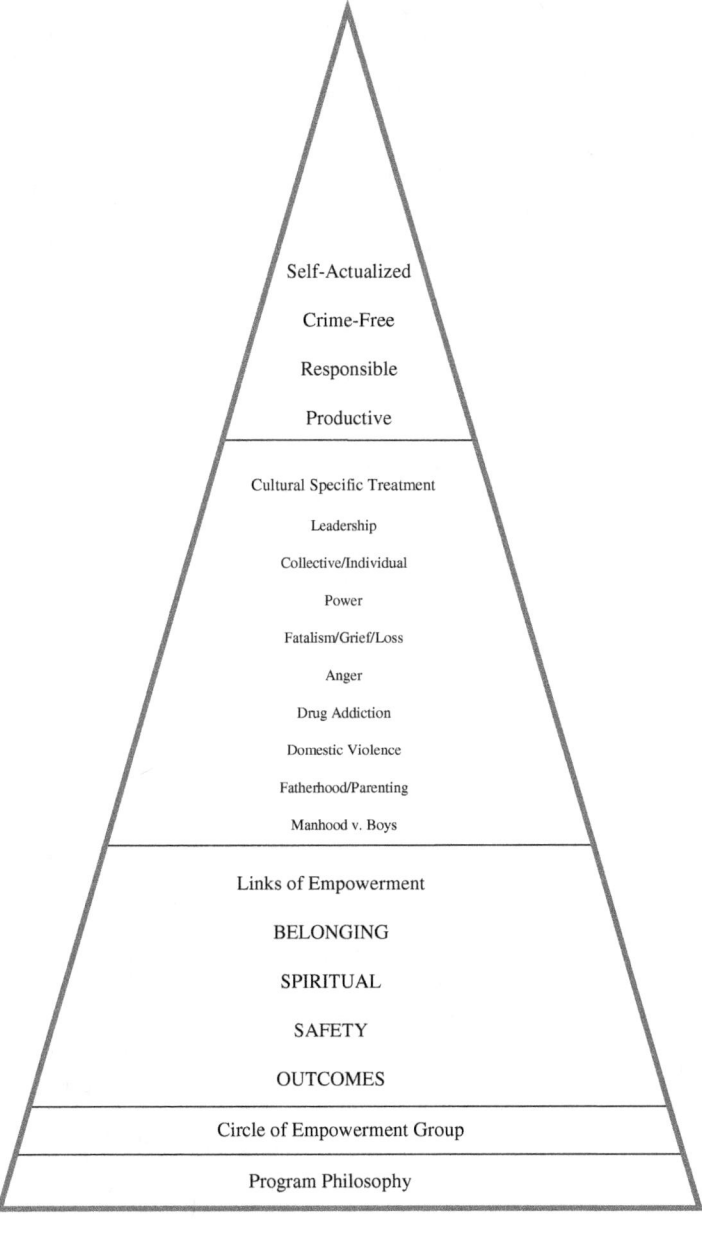

Self-Actualized

Crime-Free

Responsible

Productive

Cultural Specific Treatment

Leadership

Collective/Individual

Power

Fatalism/Grief/Loss

Anger

Drug Addiction

Domestic Violence

Fatherhood/Parenting

Manhood v. Boys

Links of Empowerment

BELONGING

SPIRITUAL

SAFETY

OUTCOMES

Circle of Empowerment Group

Program Philosophy

EPILOGUE

There have been many success stories of offenders departing the confines of prison equipped with what I refer to as the "Tool Box" for a sustained productive and crime-free lifestyle. The Tool Box consists of the four LINKS. The offender was required to sign a Pledge of Commitment, which obligated the offender to his Circle of Empowerment group in prison and the Circle Group he was joining in the community. The document was signed by me and chairperson of the Circle Group in prison. The newly released man also had to get the document signed by the chairperson of the Circle of Renewal group in the community. The chairperson of the community Circle Group provides a copy of the signed document to the chairperson of the prison group. This activity was developed to commit the man to his Circle Group in prison and to his new group in the community. It also provided encouragement to his former members in the prison group that he was continuing his commitment to the values of the Circle of Empowerment group.

One of the most successful members of a group in prison is Maurice Horton. Maurice was in prison for dealing. We met while he was at one of the minimum institutions. He was in his early twenties and participating in the group when the chairperson position became vacant. I am normally involved in the selection of a chairperson with input from the group. While he was not a group member, I think primarily because of his age, I chose him as chairperson.

In Maurice I saw tremendous potential, integrity and goodness. He was spiritually grounded. His remarks in the group were practical, empathic, and positive and spoke to personal responsibility and goal setting. He demonstrated leadership qualities with humility. He was seasoned well beyond his years. He was able to decipher the situation and extract meaningful lessons and deliver it to the men empathically. He was one with the men's positive characteristics. Basically it was divine intervention that connected my spirit with Maurice, and we have been kindred spirits ever since.

He became the chairperson of the group, and under his leadership the group increased its numbers and activities. It wrote the articles for its newsletter to share with its members and other offenders. They even shared the newsletter with family and friends.

Maurice will share with you his experience in the Circle and how he utilized its principles and values to shape his new life in prison and in the community.

My Life and Story of Circle of Recovery

My life with the Circle of Recovery was a great help while being incarcerated. Back in 1996 as someone from a good family, I had no idea I would ever see this place. My mother always told me, "A hard head would make a soft behind," and she was right. Nevertheless, my mother was never in my life. I was raised up by my grandmother, who I called "Mom."

Living in the south, my grandmother couldn't continue to deal with the racism and Separation, so we moved to

Chicago. I came to Chicago with my grandmother to a city that taught young black men to be hustlers and pimps. These stories were told on a daily basis, so in my mind I wasn't sure what a real man was anymore.

Living in Chicago was tough. Confusion and poverty was everywhere. Trying to survive the jungle of life, I continued to try to stay focused. I walked to school daily with faith that I'd one day leave this place. I continued to strive for excellence regardless of my circumstances. In 1986, I graduated from George W. Collins High School at seventeen and was accepted to Trinity Christian College in Palos Heights, Illinois. I was very proud of this accomplishment considering the hand I was dealt. Growing up in K-Town, drugs, gangs, guns, and prostitution were an everyday norm for the 'hood. Yes, and after two years of college, finally I became one of the norms; I started selling drugs searching for a quick way to leave the 'hood. But of course it ended with me getting caught and getting thirty months of probation for selling PCP.

Right after being caught my troubles of searching for a good life continued to grow. A friend of mine moved to Wisconsin and invited me up. So I took the opportunity to leave a city of darkness and poverty looking for a new beginning. When entering Wisconsin, I knew things would change for me, so I thought. My old ideas of getting rich quick came back to visit, and I politely let them in. In one year I was facing the same issues in Wisconsin that I had in Chicago—not seeking out employment but looking for the quick fix. This kind of thinking landed me in the Wisconsin prison system.

While in prison I had the opportunity to meet Mr. Jerry Smith, who at that time was the parole commissioner for the State of Wisconsin. I met him coming from my dorm, and he invited me to attend a session. When the session was over, Mr. Smith asked me to chair the group, and I accepted the offer. I had nothing in prison to cling to, so I turned to the Circle of Recovery. The Circle of Recovery was the one thing I had been missing all my life. That was how to be a real man and support my family. This group at Thompson Correctional started with four men and grew to about thirty-four before I left. Every day men would discuss their fears of being a man and picking up the torch in society. Mr. Smith would often come to the group to share his wisdom with men who had no idea of how to be a man or where to start.

What he saw was a lost group of African American men who needed to be turned around immediately before leaving prison. He knew if this concept could be embedded in their hearts, they would have a better chance of not returning to prison. We were also taught how to love our brother and support him in time of pain. After leaving prison, I took the opportunity I had from the Circle and put it into use.

The Circle of Recovery was also a program that gave me hope in my time of need. I felt joy and relief talking to the other brothers who were in the same predicament I was. The Circle wasn't just another program. It was different; it brought us closer together as one. Without us knowing it, the Circle of Recovery had started to work and the change process had begun. My experience with the Circle was great. I began to look at myself and deal with my demons one at a time. I knew if I could get past the excuses of being a man, then a change would come. Mr. Smith encouraged us to take a stand for being a man. I listened and succeeded in being a real man.

Finally, my time has come. I have been the supervisor of the Gang/Crime Diversion Taskforce in Racine, Wisconsin for ten years. This program allowed my past to build my future. I've represented this program all over the United States with respect and honor. I also started my own consultant firm Why Gangs, LLC in October 2005. I have my wife Kimberly Horton of fourteen years and four beautiful children.

Special thanks to Mr. Smith for supporting my dreams and hopes throughout my prison term. May God bless him and keep him with love.

Sincerely
Maurice Horton

The experience with the Circle Groups and my tenure in the Wisconsin Department of Corrections provided me the seeds to create the strength-based empowerment theory. My extensive research and readings have helped me formulate the LINKS of Empowerment. I have continued to refine this work through continued research, readings, and presentations to such groups as the American Correctional Association - 2002 Winter Conference and the 2006 African American Mental Health Conference sponsored by the Los Angeles Department of Mental Health.

I am asked many times how did I get such a group started in a corrections system and how did non-African American inmates blend into a group dominated by African Americans. I give credit to the Creator and the ancestors who opened the minds and hearts of corrections management to offer this program to their population.

The model is based on the collective of human decency and dignity, love, oneness and commonality of purpose. These are themes that permeate the process and principles. We constantly talked about and recommitted ourselves to loving each other in the community the same way we did in the group. New members sometimes, both African American and white, would raise the issue of different groups and the core being African American culture and history. Once I oriented the group on the principles and values of the group, the inmates could respond to these inquires.

They would inform the inquirer that everyone can learn from history, and it is their responsibility to embrace the parts that they feel can assist them in becoming fully actualized to live a crime-free lifestyle and be a productive member in their family and of society. In the Circle we believe everyone is a creation of the Creator, but we are socialized differently through culture and rules of society. We feel we can connect on a spiritual level through common values that enable each of us to perform positively and productively in consistent ways.

History provides all of us lessons on how to live in harmony with each other as well as lessons that create and sustain hate, destruction, dominance, cruelty, injustice, war and death. History also shows hope and determination against the odds.

I now live in California where I see a massive prison complex that is consumed with containment and a trickling of rehabilitation. The politicians, the criminal justice system, and the criminals are engulfed in this web of existence that only produces a modicum of sustainable progress. The newspapers are riddled with crime after crime. The television morning, mid-day and nightly news prominently telecast the lenity of crime highlighted by what Kimm refers to as the "ghetto bird," the helicopters used by law enforcement.

While I feel we are in an era of confusion and reverse logic, I see a sign of hope that some people really get what is going on. I feel the strength-based empowerment theory provides real hope and sustainable results when coupled with family and community reintegration efforts. I am optimistic about the opportunities the program provides to all three parties caught in the web, as well as communities across America.

I will leave you with a letter from inmates who have written Kimm and me following our presentations on strength-based empowerment theory and on how inmates can live a responsible and productive lifestyle free of crime.

Offender from the Green Bay Correctional Institution, Green Bay, Wisconsin Challenges and Possibilities Group
(Revised with proper grammar and punctuation for readability of reader)

I truly would like to thank you for the message delivered, not only to the group but also to the depth of my soul.

The day began with a bang when you brought to our attention and understanding the term "social amnesia." It woke me up from bad feelings related to personal issues. It unlocked some doors I had closed because I never wanted to face what was behind them. I feel I now have the courage to unlock these doors, to face my failures and to work on my trampled emotions.

I was even considering dropping from group. However, I feel very fortunate that I heard your presentation because I was moved by everything that transpired during your presentation.

Today I was in turmoil with myself over personal issues and the direction I was going to take. I was mostly affected when you asked us to look at our faults and the faults of others close to us, primarily our family and friends. For years I have blamed my mother for my station in life. You helped me understand my mom's short comings. While cruel to me, they affected my mom's ability to be all she could be as a mom. I recognize how much of this blaming of my mom and others has consumed me and helped me rationalize my irresponsible actions.

I thank you for opening up my heart to my responsibility and most importantly, for opening up my heart to forgiving, especially myself and Mom. I will always remember your words.

I believe that every inmate needs a dose of this message to complete their path or mission toward change. I really sat up and racked my mind when we were asked to close our eyes and think about who talks to us when we are alone in our cells and what are they saying.

You really made me open my eyes to see my behavior and its impact. You also gave me hope. I understand from your presentation that as long as I have hope, I have a way out of this madness.

AFTERWORD

People in prison both in their own minds and hearts have very similar experiences. They repeat the stressful thoughts from the past. They project these thoughts onto the future and it becomes prison. Thinking about things that you can no longer change only makes the mind weak. The mind keeps searching for someone to blame for the conditions that we live under. We obsess with the thought that if this or that had only happened my life would have been different. We as Americans do not believe in perfection although it is all around us if we notice.

Being trapped in your thoughts is pure suffering. Nothing can get in and nothing can get out. The doors are locked. Therapy or medication cannot infiltrate the prison of thoughts. There is a constant comparison of good and bad, right and wrong, black and white, ahead and behind, having more or less. This prison attaches to every cell in our body and causes disease or dis-ease…

A new wave of consciousness is pressing people to examine this prison of thoughts and take their mind back. Take their essence back, start to unravel the distortions and make some sense out of what is right in front of you.

As I reflect on the times we worked numerous hours on the strength-based empowerment theory, riding back and forward to the prisons where we tried out our thoughts and exercises, it became so evident to me that love was at the core of this work. When I looked into the eyes of the men I saw my son, brother and father. We were family and it was obvious I could do nothing but love them. Jerry had dedicated his career and life to this population and it was reflective in his continued committed to try and set an example as well as guide the men in their thinking.

On one occasion out of many when we were at Green Bay Correctional Institution, Jerry started the process that day with a discussion with them men on how their brains work and how these messages in their brain directed their behavior. We had worked for endless hours on our presentation using power point with music and word and poetry and lecture. He used examples from his life where his thoughts guided him to do behaviors that he later regretted. The men were glued to his every word, almost coming out of their seats. He looked into them and at them. He laughed with them, challenged their thinking, and asked them questions while teaching them the importance of their thoughts. He was more than a gift. He was the friend that they always wished for and the father and role model they never had. His "grip" on them was powerful.

When he moved the discussion to the definition of a mature man, he used the white board to write down their thoughts so that they could see them. He made a list one side for a man another side for a boy. He had them focus on the type of father they wanted and put those things under the side for man. He asked them to dream about what they could be, how starting today they could be a better husband, father, son, brother. He wrote those things down. These lessons were invaluable. The men were asking questions and telling their stories of fear, guilt and amends. Jerry led them in talking about how they can forgive themselves while commencing a new way of life, starting from the present moment—the only moment we have. I enjoyed these sessions because they reminded me of how I could be different in the moment and how I should be more accepting and loving. I had to look at my motives for doing this work in the prisons and remind myself that I was in my own prison of past thoughts even though I had a small stream of light every now and then.

As the mental health professional I was gifted to see the men change in the process and gifted with the opportunity to touch them and love them in ways that showed little fear. I was honored to have their attention and to be able to share the space with them. I was eager to learn from them and experience their thoughts as they poured out. This was not a one-way conversation. This was an interaction between people that loved each other. Their wisdom was no less important than mine and in the situation their wisdom was all that was important. When we come to people with I am smarter than you, the message is very difficult to hear and it reinforces that something is wrong with them that is an ancient thought dragged forward. The goal was to inspire them to know that the wisdom lives inside of them and it awaits their call.

Jerry and I modeled the communication process between couples and demonstrated our love for each other for them to witness. We talked about our loyalty to our marriage and the importance of being able to share even the hardest topics. I was always amazed when they said things like I wish for a relationship like that. I never knew couples could be loyal and mean it. It was important for us to communicate with them in this way.

We discussed how to live in prison without being reactive to the petty thoughts of others, on what to focus and what to leave alone. We talked about snitching and the unwritten laws that govern their conversations. We discussed the power structure that they created in their minds and lived out in their hearts. Using the Links of Empowerment we would focus on the links and the elements that made up the links, defining and redefining words and concepts that are essential to the theory. Belonging was always a core of this work, since that is our true nature to belong to each other.

When we first developed the program we focused on the needs of the African American males since their numbers in prison are overwhelming, feeling responsible for who and what they become as good elders do. We research African American and African history. We studied the concepts and elements found in the culture and worked those concepts into what we called "African center thought." The men had to work through generations of culture based on self hate.

The focus of the work was driven by examining the best in the culture, emphasizing it and exploring the contributions to the world that the African Americans culture has contributed and using this as a stepping stone and a witness to all the perfection that exist. In no way does it discount other cultures or make them bad or even judge them in any way. It explores and extracts goodness and awakens that spirit. We do realize that the world is really just one people that have been separated by many things—it is hard to keep track. We also realize that self love is based on the being the witness to love in every face you see. Our goal was to start with the face in the mirror. Love everything that you notice including the cultures and ethnic group from which you come. Learn about your history; understand the power that you share with generations.

We are of the mindset that we must learn that many things were done for us before we arrived and how someone cared about our life and sacrificed for our life. We want the men to pass the good forward; belong to those who have passed and become responsible for those yet born. We use the links to help the men see the responsibility of the past and future, and how to direct actions that supports this kind of living.

We invite the men to be present in the moment. Many of us have yet to experience because we are poisoned by the thoughts of the past. Racism separates us from others. It reinforces us to see others as less than so that we can feel more than. It limits are scope of people and reduces them to their ethnic group. We are so much more than the ethnic group from which we come. We encourage the men to see themselves as the world full of grace and GOD.

Many men from various cultural backgrounds and religions were in the groups. They learned the same lessons and translated the concepts to themselves. We encouraged all to participate; the only requirement was a willingness to learn and teach.

Racism affects all of us negatively, we all have it. It is the inability to face ourselves; to witness ourselves while we see everyone through that projection. As we see ourselves we project that on the world and to others. Once you love yourself it becomes impossible to see anything else but love in others.

When I worked with individual men, I would ask the other men to close their eyes and focus their thoughts on the subject. I remember a Latino man describing his mother as making him deal dope. He talked about being in prison because she put the first bag of dope in his hands to sell when he was 15. He described his hatred for her. He told me that he had gone to the all the prisons programs but he was not able to do anything with this thought of hatred. I talked to him about the gift he gave me to lead him into a process of forgiveness and talked about his role in selling dope and how he really hated himself. I had him close his eyes and talk to me as if I was his mother and the tears rolled down many eyes in the room that day. I told him to forgive her and set himself free. To live in the present moment, stop the reruns of thoughts from the past. The past is over never to return, take hold of his life now where he has the power. I talked to him as if I was his mother who gave him his first bag of dope, reminding him that I could only do what I had in me. I was not capable of anything else and that in the bottom of my heart I wanted more for him and I hope that he would stop and get himself into something better and show me that he was better. I described my love and asked his forgiveness. I was amazed with the stories of forgiveness this exercise evoked with the men, all the ego driven identities dropped and what we witnessed was human sorrow for the mistakes made. They were not the only ones transformed. Jerry and I could not even speak to each other on the way home.

What we learned was that the men felt they were in a safe place where they could participate in an exercise that helped them get in touch with their greatness guided by facilitators that truly believed in them and capable of being in their celebration.

The Links of Empowerment is a powerful tool when the person delivering the message has an open heart and truly believes in themselves and others. No matter how great the curriculum the presenter is the instrument and it is through their open heart and mind that the links come alive.

The more we worked on the exercises the better the men seemed to get. At Oshkosh Drug treatment facility we were asked to do a session with the drug addicts. I have worked extensively with drug addicts and was happy to see if we could create some Links of Empowerment exercises to meet their needs.

It is my experience that many drug users are not in touch with their feelings because they are so numbed out on chemicals. They are experts on not loving themselves and deflecting the blame of their circumstances on others. I wanted to see if the love lesson was as powerful as I imaged it was.

We were escorted to the housing unit where we would give our presentation. The men were gathered in their meeting area, segregated by race and power. This was beautiful and expected.

I spoke first at this event introducing concepts of being able to see beyond what is right in front of you. I have used this material many times before. This group was open and receptive. I offered them an invitation out of their limited thinking. Out of the ghost town of thoughts that imprison them in ways that is far worst than what their bodies are experiencing in the moment.

I asked them who is talking to you that you are not listening to. Who loves you and wants the best for you? What are they saying? It took a few minutes to get someone to talk but when he did it was great. He talked about this grandmother who he frequently got money from and stayed with during his addiction. He said that this was what she was saying: "Honey this will end soon and you will realize that you should have been doing something else and it will be alright. You can change. You can take control of your life. I will never give up on you. I pray for you each day that God sends you special blessings. I will have all of my friends pray for you and I will love you always." He said that she never judged him, always accepted his poor decisions and behavior, and was a rock in this life.

He said that he wanted to show her that he is clean now and that he will be getting out soon. He plans to continue his treatment and take care all of things that are needed fixing around her house. Each person except for one man had a story to tell about a person or persons in their lives that were standing with them, right or wrong. Finding love this way is amazing.

What are the stressful thoughts that keep you from loving yourself? This question starts on the path to investigating truths from fiction. Many things that we have held as beliefs are not true. No one ever loved me? Not true. I am not good enough? Not true. I am worthless. Not true. I will never stop using. Not true. Even if you have to die you will stop using one day. My wife had an affair on me; well did you have an affair on her as well? Was the drug more important than her? Yes. My children hate me. Not true children always want their parents back no matter what, even if it is not in their best interest.

This process of self examination goes on for an hour or so. Looking at thought after thought realizing that none of them are true; getting us back on track and into reality. The love exercise is in the Belonging link connected to self reflection, responsibility for self and others, having an open mind, able to see the support that you have all around you, and never being alone except in our own mind.

We closed this session with asking them to close their eyes and think of what being loved by others means to you, and think about what being loved by yourself means to you. Tell us what you see. These are the things they said:

I am free from being a follower.
I am happy to express my love back.
I can talk to wife and children instead of yell and argue.

I am sitting in my house helping my sons do their homework.

I am going to Narcotic Anonymous meetings knowing that I am not alone in my struggle.

I am safe in the world.

I can fail and try again, and again.

Each morning I wake up I begin again.

The list goes on and on. We write this list down; take them home and type it up for the men to have later to look at and review. It's like a dream board, a reminder of their dreams. Many of them can see beyond the prison walls and talk about reading books and learning new skills each day that will enable them to be a better citizen on the outside.

In conclusion, the Links of Empowerment was a celebration of self love-the love of African people around the world which means all people. The links are like pebbles that show us the way back to a more peaceful sense of self. A more truth way to be in the world, it stops the separation between people and provides a broader context for self acceptance, the only acceptance we can have.

As I struggle to let this work take its place in the world I am reminded that we are all perfectly created in GOD's image, it is what it is. I love what we were able to create and the loving moments it gave us and will continue to give us as we share it with the world. It is my hope that we hold forgiveness in our hearts for our self and others, and that we share what we have both materially and spiritually gained. Each individual act changes the world. Ashate!

ENDNOTES

1   Wilson, Amos. The Falsification of Afrikan Consciousness: Eurocentric History, Psychiatry and the Politics of White Supremacy Falsification of African Consciousness (Brooklyn: Afrikan World Infosystems.) June 1993

2   Akbar, Namin. Breaking the Psychological Chains of Slavery, Tallahassee (Florida: Mind Productions & Associates, Inc.) August 1996.

3   Mea Meares, Tracey, and Dan Kahan.. "Law and (norms of) order in the inner city." Law & Society Review. 1998. 804-838

4   Fourth Annual White Privilege Conference (April 11, 2003) in Pella, Iowa

5   Jawanza Kujufu, State of Emergency: We Must Save African American Males (Chicago:African American Images) September 1, 2001

6   Carter G. Woodson, Mis-education of the Negro. (Trenton: Africa World Press) 1st Africa World Press Edition (1990)

7   The Covenant with Black America (Chicago: Third World Press) 2006

8   African American classics in Criminology & Criminal Justice, Introduction, The Colonial Model As A Theoretical Explanation of Crime and Delinquency

9   Howard University Institute for Urban Affairs and published in their Urban Research Review, Vol.6, No.1, 1980.

10   Haki R. Madhubuti, Black Men, Obsolete, Single and Dangerous: The Afrikan American Family in Transition (Chicago: Third World Press) 1990

11   Amos N. Wilson, Black on Black Violence—The Psychodynamics of Black-Annihilation in Service of White Domination (Brooklyn: Afrikan World Infosystems.) June 1993

12   Amos N. Wilson Wilson, The Falsification of Afrikan Consciousness: Eurocentric History, Psychiatry and the Politics of White Supremacy (Brooklyn: Afrikan World Infosystems) 1993. 23

13   Na'Im Akbar ,Breaking The Chains of Psychological Slavery (Tallahassee. Mind Productions & Associates, Inc.) Fourth Printing. November 2002. 29

14   Dr. Gloria Johnson Powell, Associate Dean for Faculty, University of Wisconsin Medical School, People with Mental Illness and Substance Abuse Issues in Criminal Justice: Promising Practices in Collaborative Interventions

15   Thomas A. Parham ,Counseling Persons of African Descent - Multicultural Aspects of Counseling And Psychotherapy(Thousand Oaks: Sage Publications) March 19, 2002. 95.

16   Thomas A. Parham ,Counseling Persons of African Descent - Multicultural Aspects of Counseling And Psychotherapy (Thousand Oaks: Sage Publications) March 19, 2002

17   Marimba Ani, YURUGU: An African-Centered Critique of European Cultural Thought and Behavior (Trenton: Africa World Press) March 1994

18   Marimba Ani, YURUGU: An African-Centered Critique of European Cultural Thought and Behavior (Trenton: Africa World Press) March 1994

19   Leonard Barrett, Soul-Force: African Heritage in Afro-American Religion (Garden City, N.J.: Doubleday) 1974. 6

20   Wilson, Amos. The Falsification of Afrikan Consciousness: Eurocentric History, Psychiatry and the Politics of White Supremacy (Brooklyn: Afrikan World Infosystems) 1993

21   Thomas A. Parham, Joseph L. White, Adisa Ajamu, The Psychology of Blacks-An African Centered Perspective (Upper Saddle River: Prentice Hall) , Third Edition, 1999.

22   Thomas A. Parham, Joseph L. White, Adisa Ajamu, The Psychology of Blacks-An African Centered Perspective (Upper Saddle River: Prentice Hall) , Third Edition, 1999.107.

23   Thomas A. Parham, Joseph L. White, Adisa Ajamu, The Psychology of Blacks-An African Centered Perspective (Upper Saddle River: Prentice Hall) Third Edition, 1999.

24   Thomas A. Parham ,Counseling Persons of African Descent - Multicultural Aspects of Counseling And Psychotherapy (Thousand Oaks: Sage Publications) March 19, 2002

25   Wilson, Amos. The Falsification of Afrikan Consciousness: Eurocentric History, Psychiatry and the Politics of White Supremacy (Brooklyn: Afrikan World Infosystems) 1993

26   Thomas Parham, Thomas-Editor, Counseling Persons of African Descent, Raising the Bar Of Practitioner Competence (Thousand Oaks: Sage Publications) 2002 4.

27   Thomas A. Parham, Joseph L. White, Adisa Ajamu, The Psychology of Blacks-An African Centered Perspective (Upper Saddle River: Prentice Hall) Third Edition. 1999.

28   Bell Hooks, Killing Rage-Ending Racism (New York: Henry, Holt & Company, L.L.C.) 1995.

29 Thomas A. Parham, Joseph L. White, Adisa Ajamu, The Psychology of Blacks-An African Centered Perspective (Upper Saddle River: Prentice Hall) Third Edition. 1999.

30 Randall Robinson , The Reckoning: What Blacks Owe to Each Other (New York: Dutton-The Penguin Group) 2002.

31 Hillary Rodham Clinton, It Takes a Village (New York: Simon & Schuster) 1996.

32 This speech was delivered by Willie Lynch on the bank of the James River in the colony of Virginia in 1712. Lynch was a British slave owner in the West Indies. He was invited to the colony of Virginia in 1712 to teach his methods to slave owners there. The term "lynching" is derived from his last name.

33 Thomas A. Parham ,Counseling Persons of African Descent - Multicultural Aspects of Counseling And Psychotherapy (Thousand Oaks: Sage Publications) March 19, 2002

34 Thomas Parham, Thomas-Editor, Counseling Persons of African Descent, Raising the Bar Of Practitioner Competence (Thousand Oaks: Sage Publications) 2002, 4

35 Thomas Parham, Thomas-Editor, Counseling Persons of African Descent, Raising the Bar Of Practitioner Competence (Thousand Oaks: Sage Publications) 2002

36 Gary Zukav, Soul Stories (New York: Fireside) August 1, 2000

The Willie Lynch Letter: The Making Of A Slave!

This speech was delivered by Willie Lynch on the bank of the James River in the colony of Virginia in 1712. Lynch was a British slave owner in the West Indies. He was invited to the colony of Virginia in 1712 to teach his methods to slave owners there. The term "lynching" is derived from his last name.

December 25, 1712

Gentlemen:

I greet you here on the bank of the James River in the year of our Lord one thousand seven hundred and twelve. First, I shall thank you, the gentlemen of the Colony of Virginia, for bringing me here. I am here to help you solve some of your problems with slaves. Your invitation reached me on my modest plantation in the West Indies, where I have experimented with some of the newest and still the oldest methods for control of slaves. Ancient Rome's would envy us if my program is implemented.

As our boat sailed south on the James River, named for our illustrious King, whose version of the Bible we cherish, I saw enough to know that your problem is not unique. While Rome used cords of wood as crosses for standing human bodies along its highways in great numbers, you are here using the tree and the rope on occasions. I caught the whiff of a dead slave hanging from a tree, a couple miles back. You are not only losing valuable stock by hangings, you are having uprisings, slaves are running away, your crops are sometimes left in the fields too long for maximum profit, You suffer occasional fires, your animals are killed.

Gentlemen, you know what your problems are; I do not need to elaborate. I am not here to enumerate your problems, I am here to introduce you to a method of solving them. In my bag here, I have a foolproof method for controlling your black slaves. I guarantee every one of you that if installed correctly it will control the slaves for at least 300 years [2012]. My method is simple. Any member of your family or your overseer can use it. I have outlined a number of differences among the slaves and make the differences bigger. I use fear, distrust and envy for control.

These methods have worked on my modest plantation in the West Indies and it will work throughout the South. Take this simple little list of differences and think about them. On top of my list is "age" but it's there only because it starts with an "A." The second is "COLOR" or shade, there is intelligence, size, sex, size of plantations and status on plantations, attitude of owners, whether the slaves live in the valley, on a hill, East, West, North, South, have fine hair, course hair, or is tall or short. Now that you have a list of differences, I shall give you an outline of action, but before that, I shall assure you that distrust is stronger than trust and envy stronger than adulation, respect or admiration. The Black slaves after receiving this indoctrination shall carry on and will become self refueling and self generating for hundreds of years, maybe thousands. Don't forget you must pitch the old black Male vs. the young black Male, and the young black Male against the old black male. You must use the dark skin slaves vs. the light skin slaves, and the light skin slaves vs. the dark skin slaves. You must use the female vs. the male. And the male vs. the female. You must also have you white servants and overseers distrust all

Blacks. It is necessary that your slaves trust and depend on us. They must love, respect and trust only us. Gentlemen, these kits are your keys to control. Use them. Have your wives and children use them, never miss an opportunity. If used intensely for one year, the slaves themselves will remain perpetually distrustful of each other.

Thank you gentlemen

Lets Make a Slave

It was the interest and business of slave holders to study human nature, and the slave nature in particular, with a view to practical results. I and many of them attained astonishing proficiency in this direction. They had to deal not with earth, wood and stone, but with men and by every regard they had for their own safety and prosperity they needed to know the material on which they were to work. Conscious of the injustice and wrong they were every hour perpetuating and knowing what they themselves would do. Were they the victims of such wrongs? They were constantly looking for the first signs of the dreaded retribution. They watched, therefore with skilled and practiced eyes, and learned to read with great accuracy, the state of mind and heart of the slave, through his sable face. Unusual sobriety, apparent abstractions, sullenness and indifference indeed, any mood out of the common was afforded ground for suspicion and inquiry.

Let us make a slave. What do we need? First of all we need a black nigger man, a pregnant nigger woman and her baby nigger boy. Second, we will use the same basic principle that we use in breaking a horse, combined with some more sustaining factors. What we do with horses is that we break them from one form of life to another that is we reduce them from their natural state in nature. Whereas nature provides them with the natural capacity to take care of their offspring, we break that natural string of independence from them and thereby create a dependency status, so that we may be able to get from them useful production for our business and pleasure.

Cardinal Principles for making a Negro

For fear that our future Generations may not understand the principles of breaking both of the beast together, the nigger and the horse. We understand that short range planning economics results in periodic economic chaos; so that to avoid turmoil in the economy, it requires us to have breath and depth in long range comprehensive planning, articulating both skill sharp perceptions. We lay down the following principles for long range comprehensive economic planning. Both horse and niggers is no good to the economy in the wild or natural state. Both must be broken and tied together for orderly production. For orderly future, special and particular attention must be paid to the female and the youngest offspring. Both must be crossbred to produce a variety and division of labor. Both must be taught to respond to a peculiar new language. Psychological and physical instruction of containment must be created for both. We hold the six cardinal principles as truth to be self evident, based upon the following the discourse concerning the economics of breaking and tying the horse and the nigger together, all inclusive of the six principles laid down about. NOTE: Neither principle alone will suffice

for good economics. All principles must be employed for orderly good of the nation. Accordingly, both a wild horse and a wild or nature nigger is dangerous even if captured, for they will have the tendency to seek their customary freedom, and in doing so, might kill you in your sleep. You cannot rest. They sleep while you are awake, and are awake while you are asleep. They are dangerous near the family house and it requires too much labor to watch them away from the house. Above all, you cannot get them to work in this natural state. Hence both the horse and the nigger must be broken; that is breaking them from one form of mental life to another. Keep the body take the mind! In other words break the will to resist. Now the breaking process is the same for both the horse and the nigger, only slightly varying in degrees.

But as we said before, there is an art in long range economic planning. You must keep your eye and thoughts on the female and the offspring of the horse and the nigger. A brief discourse in offspring development will shed light on the key to sound economic principles. Pay little attention to the generation of original breaking, but concentrate on future generations.

Therefore, if you break the female mother, she will break the offspring in its early years of development and when the offspring is old enough to work, she will deliver it up to you, for her normal female protective tendencies will have been lost in the original breaking process. For example take the case of the wild stud horse, a female horse and an already infant horse and compare the breaking process with two captured nigger males in their natural state, a pregnant nigger woman with her infant offspring. Take the stud horse, break him for limited containment.

Completely break the female horse until she becomes very gentle, whereas you or anybody can ride her in her comfort.

Breed the mare and the stud until you have the desired offspring. Then you can turn the stud to freedom until you need him again. Train the female horse where by she will eat out of your hand, and she will in turn train the infant horse to eat out of your hand also. When it comes to breaking the uncivilized nigger, use the same process, but vary the degree and step up the pressure, so as to do a complete reversal of the mind. Take the meanest and most restless nigger, strip him of his clothes in front of the remaining male niggers, the female, and the nigger infant, tar and feather him, tie each leg to a different horse faced in opposite directions, set him a fire and beat both horses to pull him apart in front of the remaining nigger. The next step is to take a bull whip and beat the remaining nigger male to the point of death, in front of the female and the infant. Don't kill him, but put the fear of God in him, for he can be useful for future breeding.

The Breaking Process of the African Woman

Take the female and run a series of tests on her to see if she will submit to your desires willingly. Test her in every way, because she is the most important factor for good economics. If she shows any sign of resistance in submitting completely to your will, do not hesitate to use the bull whip on her to extract that last bit of resistance out of her. Take care not to kill her, for in doing so, you spoil good economic. When in complete submission, she will train her off springs in the early years to submit to labor when the become of age. Understanding is the best thing. Therefore, we shall go deeper into this area of the subject matter concerning what we have produced here in this breaking process of the female nigger.

We have reversed the relationship in her natural uncivilized state she would have a strong dependency on the uncivilized nigger male, and she would have a limited protective tendency toward her independent male offspring and would raise male off springs to be dependent like her. Nature had provided for this type of balance. We reversed nature by burning and pulling a civilized nigger apart and bull whipping the other to the point of death, all in her presence. By her being left alone, unprotected, with the male image destroyed, the ordeal caused her to move from her psychological dependent state to a frozen independent state. In this frozen psychological state of independence, she will raise her male and female offspring in reversed roles.

For fear of the young males life she will psychologically train him to be mentally weak and dependent, but physically strong. Because she has become psychologically independent, she will train her female off springs to be psychological independent. What have you got? You've got the nigger women out front and the nigger man behind and scared. This is a perfect situation of sound sleep and economic. Before the breaking process, we had to be alertly on guard at all times.

Now we can sleep soundly, for out of frozen fear his woman stands guard for us. He cannot get past her early slave molding process. He is a good tool, now ready to be tied to the horse at a tender age. By the time a nigger boy reaches the age of sixteen, he is soundly broken in and ready for a long life of sound and efficient work and the reproduction of a unit of good labor force. Continually through the breaking of uncivilized savage nigger, by throwing the nigger female savage into a frozen psychological state of independence, by killing of the protective male image, and by creating a submissive dependent mind of the nigger male slave, we have created an orbiting cycle that turns on its own axis forever, unless a phenomenon occurs and re shifts the position of the male and female slaves. We show what we mean by example. Take the case of the two economic slave units and examine them closely.

The Nigger Marriage

We breed two nigger males with two nigger females. Then we take the nigger males away from them and keep them moving and working. Say one nigger female bears a nigger female and the other bears a nigger male. Both nigger females being without influence of the nigger male image, frozen with an independent psychology, will raise their offspring into reverse positions. The one with the female offspring will teach her to be like herself, independent and negotiable (we negotiate with her, through her, by her, we negotiate her at will). The one with the nigger male offspring, she being frozen with a subconscious fear for his life, will raise him to be mentally dependent and weak, but physically strong, in other words, body over mind. Now in a few years when these two offspring's become fertile for early reproduction we will mate and breed them and continue the cycle. That is good, sound, and long range comprehensive planning.

Warning: Possible Interloping Negatives

Earlier we talked about the non economic good of the horse and the nigger in their wild or natural state; we talked out the principle of breaking and tying them together for orderly production. Furthermore, we talked about paying particular attention to the female savage and her offspring for orderly future planning, then more recently we stated that, by reversing the positions of the male and female savages, we created an orbiting cycle that turns on its own axis forever unless a phenomenon occurred and resift and positions of the male and female savages. Our experts warned us about the possibility of this phenomenon occurring, for they say that the mind has a strong drive to correct and recorrect itself over a period of time if I can touch some substantial original historical base, and they advised us that the best way to deal with the phenomenon is to shave off the brute's mental history and create a multiplicity of phenomena of illusions, so that each illusion will twirl in its own orbit, something similar to floating balls in a vacuum.

This creation of multiplicity of phenomena of illusions entails the principle of crossbreeding the nigger and the horse as we stated above, the purpose of which is to create a diversified division of labor thereby creating different levels of labor and different values of illusion at each connecting level of labor. The results of which is the severance of the points of original beginnings for each sphere illusion. Since we feel that the subject matter may get more complicated as we proceed in laying down our economic plan concerning the purpose, reason and effect of crossbreeding horses and nigger, we shall lay down the following definition terms for future generations.

Orbiting cycle means a thing turning in a given path. *Axis* means upon which or around which a body turns. *Phenomenon* means something beyond ordinary conception and inspires awe and wonder. *Multiplicity* means a great number. Sphere means a globe. *Cross breeding a horse* means taking a horse and breeding it with an ass and you get a dumb backward ass long headed mule that is not reproductive nor productive by itself.

Crossbreeding niggers mean taking so many drops of good white blood and putting them into as many nigger women as possible, varying the drops by the various tone that you want, and then letting them breed with each other until another cycle of color appears as you desire. What this means is this; Put the niggers and the horse in a breeding pot, mix some assess and some good white blood and what do you get? You got a multiplicity of colors of ass backward, unusual niggers, running, tied to a backward ass long headed mule, the one productive of itself, the other sterile. (The one constant, the other dying, we keep the nigger constant for we may replace the mules for another tool) both mule and nigger tied to each other, neither knowing where the other came from and neither productive for itself, nor without each other.

Control the Language

Crossbreeding completed, for further severance from their original beginning, we must completely annihilate the mother tongue of both the new nigger and the new mule and institute a new language that involves the new life's work of both.

You know language is a peculiar institution. It leads to the heart of a people. The more a foreigner knows about the language of another country the more he is able to move through all levels of that society. Therefore, if the foreigner is an enemy of the country, to the extent that he knows the body of the language, to that extent is the country vulnerable to attack or invasion of a foreign culture. For example, if you take a slave, if you teach him all about your language, he will know all your secrets, and he is then no more a slave, for you can't fool him any longer. For example, if you told a slave that he must perform in getting out "our crops" and he knows the language well, he would know that "our crops" didn't mean "our crops" and the slavery system would break down, for he would relate on the basis of what "our crops" really meant. So you have to be careful in setting up the new language for the slaves would soon be in your house, talking to you "man to man" and that is death to our economic system. In addition, the definitions of words or terms are only a minute part of the process. Values are created and transported by communication through the body of the language. A total society has many interconnected value system. All the values in the society have bridges of language to connect them for orderly working in the society. But for these language bridges, these many value systems would sharply clash and cause internal strife or civil war, the degree of the conflict being determined by the magnitude of the issues or relative opposing strength in whatever form.

For example, if you put a slave in a hog pen and train him to live there and incorporate in him to value it as a way of life completely, the biggest problem you would have out of him is that he would worry you about provisions to keep the hog pen clean, or the same hog pen and make a slip and incorporate something in his language where by he comes to value a house more than he does his hog pen, you got a problem. He will soon be in your house.

www.ingramcontent.com/pod-product-compliance
Lightning Source LLC
Chambersburg PA
CBHW060622290526
45793CB00001B/105